Diary of an Ex-Insomniac

Copyright © Nicki Gillard 2017

First Edition

Published by Oswald Badger

ISBN number 978-1548318512

All rights reserved

Nicki Gillard has asserted her right under the Copyright, Designs and Patents Act 1988 to be identified as the author of this work. This book is sold subject to the condition that it shall not, by way of trade or otherwise be resold, hired out, or circulated, in any other way without the author's prior consent.

Cover design by John Gillard

Nicki Gillard

Diary of an Ex-Insomniac

Introducing the Insomnia
DITCH-AND-SWITCH®

Contents

Part One: Ditch and Switch		1
1	Life as an insomniac	3
2	Eureka – ditch insomnia	13
3	Everything's alright	21
4	Being awake	30
Part Two: Growing the mindset		39
5	A product that works	40
6	Practising the mindset	51
7	Ex-insomniac skills	63
8	Alter my angle	74
Part Three: For day-to-day living		85
9	Connections	86
10	Challenge	97

11	Creative energy	113
12	Life and story	129

Part Four: For life's ups and downs — **141**

13	Positive about uncertainty	142
14	Equilibrium	161
15	The possibility of change	184
16	Sustainable path	202

End note 1	215
End note 2	230
End note 3	232

I had been trapped in the vicious circle of stress and insomnia for a long time. Then suddenly I discovered the Ditch-and-Switch.

This book, or memoir, tells you how that came about. It tells you how I ditched the horrible stress of insomnia for good.

It's about how I ditched being trapped and switched to being free.

I invite anyone who has stress in their life (I think that covers everyone) to read from my diary with its struggles and discoveries. If you will allow me to share my ideas with you, then you can decide for yourself if there is anything in my journey that can help you with yours.

Enjoy the read.

Nicki Gillard

Part One
Ditch and Switch

I begin with a snippet from my diary. I'd scrawled it after a sleepless night.

So not a happy start to the book – but it has to be there to show you how bad my insomnia was.

You saw from the title that I did get over it and in Part One I'll tell you how.

1
Life as an insomniac

The vicious circle

Horrible horrible night – right back to the beginning with the revolting insomnia frustration anger feeling awful anxious about the next day about being able to cope with doing everything but not wanting to cancel Just like last summer – horrible horrible night after night insomnia set in – no way out of it I've tried so hard to get over it and now I'm back to square one – can't believe it Can't face going through it all again – can't put in that much effort again – can't do it Such an enormous drag – so fed up and annoyed about it why can't the results be permanent?

I was a chronic insomniac when I wrote that in my diary. As you know, I'm an ex-insomniac now. I was in a horrible self-perpetuating loop then. The vicious circle of insomnia had started a full 10 years before. I still remember the exact start of it, the very first time I had a completely sleepless night. Yes, I remember it very well. These are my memories of it:

I was living for a while in a flat on the seventh floor of a block in Kemptown. It had great sea views. I was reading in bed (the book was The Secret History by Donna Tartt) and fell nicely asleep. Then I was jolted awake by the telephone ringing on the bedroom extension. It was 1 o'clock in the morning and a cheery girl was calling her friend for a chat. I explained she didn't live there now. I didn't get to sleep again after that. I was awake all night and still awake as morning came. I hadn't slept when it was time to get up for work. I was a teacher then. That was the start of my chronic insomnia.

The vicious circle goes like this. You are awake. You should be asleep. You need your sleep for the day ahead. You must not be stressed about being awake, or you will not sleep. But not sleeping is worrying. The time goes on and it gets worse. Now you have insomnia.

That first day of many after a sleepless night I tried hard not to let the insomnia affect me. It was the start of a long period of trying. Each night I tried to sleep. I did that for a whole term of teaching, a term of sleepless nights. Then it was the summer break. I never slept, a holiday of sleepless nights. Finally chronic insomnia curtailed my teaching career.

I didn't have a way out of it as I have now. I wasn't aware of my insomniac thinking. I was caught up inside the vicious circle – I couldn't see it from the outside, so I had no chance of jumping out of it. A decade later, not long after the *horrible horrible night*, I discovered I could be in the (infinitely preferable) ex-insomniac virtuous circle instead.

The vicious circle is about mindset. The virtuous circle is too.

But – you might well ask – how can you relax when you have to get up for work? Not sleeping is worrying. How do you not worry?

My answer: By taking charge of your mindset.

It's all about your attitude to being awake – you have a mindset choice. For a start you can let go of trying to sleep.

What does it mean anyway: trying to sleep? It's meaningless. You can't make yourself sleep (and nobody else can either). But you don't need to. Your body will take care of sleep, so you don't have to concern yourself with it at all. If you're awake, resting is fine.

Try it. It works. This simple idea over time got me out of being an insomniac for good. I will tell you more about how it is possible to get out of the stressful trying to sleep and into the restful leaving it to your body – that is my aim in writing this book.

The jump from the vicious to the virtuous circle is my own practical solution. The jump was instant when the turning-point came, but I'd got to it oh-so gradually. When I looked back through my diaries I could see the solution evolving. I'll take you through it – how not to have insomnia.

Insomnia does not exist

To me it was an entity in itself. It existed. Insomnia was so real that once it made an appearance:

The door was ajar and let in enough light for me to make out, not far from my bed, a griffin insinuating itself into the room. This was my insomnia, manifested as a moving, living creature with face and eyes.

I pulled the duvet up against my chin, and shut the creature out of my eyes. I opened them again to confirm the hallucination gone, but found, instead, it had developed more form and was squeezing this into the room. It moved like a snake but more rolling than writhing. Now sliding over the top of the door, it was swimming on the surface of the air, looking around, making ready to feast on the space.

No, I would not allow this figment into my sight. I chose to keep it shut out. I moved my thoughts around the room, knowing it would still be there if I opened my eyes. So all night, while people everywhere were sleeping, I did this musing, not-looking thing, thinking blind around the room, covering every detail. I was prepared to go on as long as it took.

After an unspecifiable length of time I saw in my mind's eye random specks of light through tiny holes in the curtains. Still, I kept my eyes shut for fear of reconnecting with the insomnia griffin. After silent debate with myself I agreed to wait until I was sure it was morning, wait for signs of the rest of the world waking up, before I allowed myself to see again.

Back then I had the mindset of an insomniac. I knew insomnia existed. I was a rational person, but there was no way of getting away from the reality of it when I experienced it so intensely. And it would never go away.

Insomnia gets its claws into you. It grinds away at you and spoils everything you want to enjoy. It gnaws into your core. You know it's dictating who you are, but there's nothing you can do about it. It is inescapable, claustrophobic, and intolerable.

Sleep is a prized possession. It is unattainable, precious as gold, and out of your reach. It slips away so easily. It is the most desirable commodity, yet every other person in the world takes it for granted.

You are desperate for sleep. You need it, you desire it. You had it once, but you lost it. It comes back to you occasionally, but only to taunt you, before it runs away from you again.

In its place you are left with something real and tangible, not fleeting like sleep; you are left with 'Insomnia'. It has a will of its own, nothing to do with you. And it's frightening.

I remember how insidious it was. I would think I was over it and sleeping fine. But there was always the threat of a relapse. It could happen at any time, out of the blue. When it struck, I would search for causes or triggers, but in the end there was no rhyme or reason to it.

A relapse could be brief, or insomnia could set in. I never knew which it was going to be. The insomnia had a mind of its own. I was at its mercy.

You can never get used to this insomnia feeling – it's different from not sleeping well. Not sleeping at all – and having scenarios as sleep/dream substitutes – is doubly horrible. You start off a well person when you go to bed and end up an ill person overnight literally. It's impossible to explain to anyone what it's like. Physically you ache too. If you are in the same position for hours and you are asleep, your body is okay with it. But when you are not sleeping, your body responds by aching all over. This includes all different areas of the head, producing a low-level skull ache. Not very nice. One of the scenarios was Mum telling me she was going to die – she said she had run out of years and wanted to go home. We cried together and I comforted her.

I would feel terrible the next day, physical illness taking over my head and my whole body. It was impossible to describe it to a person who's feeling normal, so I didn't want to even try. And yet I ached for another human being to understand and sympathise. I remember that rotten dilemma.

And there's something else I remember very well. One night my insomnia reached such a pitch it caused me to panic. It was after a long succession of nights without sleep and my despair was building up. I was overcome by a sudden, frightening awareness of being awake when I wasn't meant to be. This turned into a feeling of claustrophobia, an intolerable anxiety. Panic has a terrible momentum. You know there is no limit to where it is taking you, and that is terrifying. I was conscious of all this at the time, so it is ground into my memory.

I see it so clearly now. I was trapped in the insomniac mindset of need and fear: the need to sleep and the fear of being awake.

I'm free of that now. It doesn't matter if I'm awake – my body will decide on sleep, so I don't have to bother about it. My body aching all over was a stress response. I would never get that now – not since I ditched the vicious circle of stress and insomnia. I may be lying awake for quite some time but my body is fine with it. Resting. In the virtuous circle of confidence and control.

I am confident I don't have insomnia and never will again. For me it doesn't exist anymore.

My diary

When I started my diary I'd been out of teaching for 10 years. I was able then to work full-time on our small family business of property letting. I thought I was keeping insomnia at bay, but I knew my sleep was held by a thread. I'd have methods of getting to sleep, which sometimes worked and often didn't. I tried so hard for so long. I wanted to be positive and practical. At one point I sent for an American program with a CD of motivational statements. But solutions led me more and more into the insomnia trap. For example, at one stage I could only get to sleep if I played relaxing music with a soothing voice-over. Except that I couldn't. It only made my hold on sleep more flimsy.

And then, a decade after the original long bout, the insomnia came back worse than ever, a terrible relapse, another round of completely sleepless nights. It was in the south of France, the summer holidays, swimming pool and barbecues, and the horrible, horrible insomnia.

I'd started my diary by then. It was not a specific insomnia diary. I'd joined the Rottingdean Writers' Group and I was writing about lots of subjects and trying out different genres, including poetry and short stories. I also wrote in my notebook every morning, just everyday things.

Later, when I decided I wanted to pass on to other people how I ditched insomnia, I had to trawl through all my notebooks to find the relevant extracts. It wasn't easy, I can tell you – but I was on a mission! My mission: to convey to insomniacs how not to have insomnia – permanently.

It is all about your attitude to being awake. There are two alternatives. One mindset has insomnia, the other doesn't.

My ex-insomniac mindset evolved. I can trace that in my diary. This extract shows my attitude to the effects of not sleeping.

When Martin woke up I told him about the scenario with Mum. Feel a bit better now I have let some of it out. I will be alright today when I get going. As M just said, I won't suffer any long-term effects, never have before and won't this time. I will get dressed and go down for breakfast – get some normality back. In fact I am feeling near normal again already just from saying it.

The fixed insomnia mindset thrives on worries about not sleeping. So let's separate the myth from the facts. For a start, it won't do me any harm. It's not a fact that sleeplessness makes me ill; it doesn't. I used to think it gave me that horrible skull ache. It became my own myth to add to my repertoire of myths. What else? Hallucinating. That was a stress response. Same with aching all over. Not a problem with my body caused by insomnia.

It won't hurt me. Sleep deprivation may have been used as a torture but that's not relevant to me. I am not a torture victim, even if I do feel weird and spaced out. Knowing insomnia is not an illness is important. It helps me trust my body and relax about being awake.

The end of insomnia

When you are held in the grip of insomnia you become locked into searching for ways of getting to sleep. You look for causes and triggers. You're bound to because that seems to be the only way out. You say, "If I could only understand why I'm not sleeping, I might be able to find a way of stopping this wretched insomnia."

The doctor had signed me off teaching for a couple of weeks when I went to see a psychotherapist. This was around the time of my insomnia griffin hallucination. She told me there must be underlying stress issues. I had six sessions exploring the possibilities – within my life history and the immediate stresses of teaching. It made things more frustrating because it illuminated nothing.

Insomnia is wound up in itself, viciously self-perpetuating. The insomnia is the stress.

Right. So you want to get out of the stress of it – now. "There must be something I can do. There must be a cure out there somewhere, if I try hard enough to find it."

Yes, there are pills and therapies, treatments and programs, all designed to alleviate insomnia. I know because I tried most of them: sleeping pills, Prozac, Cognitive Behavioural Therapy, sleep programs with CDs...

I thought I was benefiting from self-help materials – at the time they seemed to be working. The trouble was that nothing ever lasted.

All insomniacs want quick fixes. "Just tell me how I can get to sleep. And if I wake up, tell me how I can get back to sleep again." That's all you need to know. End of story.

What I'm suggesting doesn't do that. This isn't a quick-fix cure for insomnia. It's not a treatment program. It's not a step-by-step guide with a start, finish and time-scale. You've probably tried some of those. You may feel you've tried just about everything. If so, you'll know lots of things work to some extent, but you'll be desperate for permanence. That's where this book comes in. It's about permanence – never having insomnia again.

I found this diary extract showing how I'd embraced the ex-insomniac mindset: insomnia didn't exist for me anymore.

Pity I didn't sleep much last night (probably 2 hours only). Ironic really that I was over-tired. Still, the main thing is my attitude to it. Nothing terrible is going to happen to me – I won't pass out or be unable to cope, and I'll rest tonight. I've been here before, physically anyway. Mentally it's different. I don't have insomnia – I did go to sleep and would have slept longer if I hadn't had to get up at 7am. So it's not a problem. As always, just get on with each task as it comes and deal with the day a step at a time.

'I don't have insomnia.' How utterly satisfying!

I'll tell you how I escaped from the trap of insomnia and stress, and how I built on the freedom of it. I'll tell you with the help of my diary.

2
Eureka – ditch insomnia

The tedium scenario

After the second major relapse I was trying even harder with my problem solving. I knew that insomnia could strike at any time. I had no control over when it struck or how severely. I was a sitting duck.

I remember I took my CD player away to Harpenden with me. I needed the relaxation track so I could get to sleep. I set up the stereo player in the lounge ready for sleeping downstairs on the sofa. How ridiculous, the loop of relaxation – more and more needed to achieve the goal of sleep that never came! But it helped me because it was obviously ridiculous.

Useful memory tags: the CD Loop and the Tedium Scenario. They mark the beginning of the end for my insomnia. It wasn't the desperation that was the turning-point for me – it was the tedium.

I was so utterly sick and tired of the whole mass of stuff I'd bought or read, abandoned or persevered with – relaxation techniques, bedtime regimes, natural remedies, theories on causes.

Then there were all those endless choices around sleep, all

those dos and don'ts: what bedding/pillow, how hot/cold you are or the room is, how light/dark the room, read/not read, watch television to relax you /beware of it over-stimulating you, how early/late it is, what food or drink you've had and how long before bedtime. Then a whole load more choices and considerations to do with your partner or others in the house.

Q. What was the turning-point?

A. A wave of tedium hit me.

Frustration creates the need for something new. After circling around in my mind, the idea was sudden in the end. Suddenly a click, a new mindset, a new take on the whole insomnia situation. I just wanted to ditch the lot. Throw out everything associated with insomnia, all the insomnia paraphernalia.

It felt like a breakthrough just thinking it because it felt like I was ditching insomnia itself. And I was.

I binned insomnia in my head. What could I bin for real? The book and CD went into the book swap. I went through the American affirmational statements crossing out counter-productive ones. I was on a roll, scouring, scoring out, scribbled sidenotes: pressure, rubbish, pressure, pressure. Affirmations 3 sheets long. I kept them for future curiosity and put the accompanying manual in the bin. Oh the joy of ditching! Insomnia in the bin. The oh-so-important sleep solutions binned along with belief in insomnia. It's so clear to me now. I'm in charge here. This material is all based on insomnia existing and it doesn't. It's a mindset choice. My choice. This is powerful.

And eminently practical. First identify what's wrong with the existing situation. Problem: there was no way out of the insomnia trap. Solution: ditch the trap. Don't have it. Eureka, I have ditched insomnia itself.

Throwing out

I'd had enough. I was ruthless and I loved it. It was like throwing out clothes you haven't worn for years but thought you had to keep. And, just as you never missed the old clothes, you find that none of those carefully honed routines around bedtime makes a scrap of difference. So ditch the lot – they're all too much trouble. What a relief when you do!

I swapped the fug of bedtime dos and don'ts for the fresh air of doing nothing and I got into the swing of it. I threw out the myths too. It's not a fact I need an 8-hour uninterrupted sleep; I don't. What's the norm for regularity and pattern of sleep? There isn't one. Does a nap on the sofa stop me sleeping in bed? No. When people tell me they fall asleep as soon as their head hits the pillow, I nod and reach for the salt (pinch of).

Still on a roll, I gave triggers the elbow too. Will it help me to sleep if I rack my brains for what caused me to be awake? No, exactly the opposite; it just keeps me looking back frustrated. Triggers and causes are part of the paraphernalia of insomnia I can dump along with quick fixes.

I was awake over several hours last night – must have got to sleep 5ish on the sofa until 8am. I knew what had probably caused it (M poured me an overly large Pina Colada!) but I also knew that identifying triggers was counter-productive (though tempting). The main thing was not to allow it to become stressful. Say, 'What does it matter? It won't do me harm. I can sleep another time. What can I usefully think about?' Or think of nothing if I prefer. It all works, and now I'm positive about the 3 hours and I'll rest as and when I get the chance, or wait till tonight if I prefer. It makes no difference – it doesn't matter. No need to think about it – when the time comes, my body will do the deciding about sleep anyway, not me.

Being awake is not insomnia.

Change names and attitudes

When I give myself the name 'insomniac' I have surrendered to the whole idea of it. I have defined myself. A multiplicity of attitudes flow from it and become embedded. I have to rid myself of the attitudes and the name in one combined bundle. I have to un-bed them. Then I can just do nothing – let my body decide about sleep.

Author's note: Un-bedding is a technical term I use for ditching, not to be confused with getting someone up in the morning.

I have made a start and un-bedding gathers momentum. I rid myself of one name and put another in its place – ex-insomniac. I create the attitudes to go with it, all at the same time.

Insomnia is not part of my life now because it doesn't fit in with my attitudes and I will never go back to it. I know this is permanent because it has come from me, not from the superficial following of advice/instructions but from a real sense that I am not an insomniac anymore.

I throw out all the unwanted stuff and I find I am making all sorts of different choices. This is the beauty of it – the choices are all entirely up to me.

Sometimes I want to use my resting-in-bed time to think about particular items before I let my body decide about sleep. If I'm awake after that I usually think about what clothes I'm going to wear next time I'm going somewhere or what clothes to pack. This grounds my thoughts (if I'm ready to ground my thoughts). I'm not trying to go to sleep. It's not a getting-to-sleep exercise. There's freedom in not having to try. If I find myself still awake, no matter. I usually consider getting up, and either this is too much trouble (and sometimes I fall asleep thinking about it) or I do get up. It's up to me whether it's just for a quick bathroom/drink of water and back to bed, or stay up longer. It doesn't matter – I don't have insomnia anymore.

Being awake is not insomnia.

Falling asleep

Q. But how does ditching insomnia get you to sleep?

A. Okay, here's a practical suggestion:

Insomnia has become an issue again – no sleep till early morning – grabbed a couple of hours and up at 7.30am. Anyway, that's better than nothing. I got a bit agitated around 4am when I hadn't slept and no prospect of sleep, but M woke up then and at first it made me more stressed by expressing my emotions to him, but then he helped me by quoting my own advice. Not to be emotional but practical, which I did and it worked. I did a 'John on the beach' to get away from my emotional response and allow myself to rest.

That's how I turned things around. "But what's this John on the beach?" you might well be asking. Here's a poem I wrote, which hopefully will explain it to you:

John on the Beach

*John's on the beach, Marseillan Plage
It should be hot, baking, boiling
After all it is the South of France*

*But it's not. It's chilly, freezing
He's been in the sea and now he's out
Towel hugged round, shivering, bivering*

*'I'm so cold I can't stop shaking'
But then – at the drop of a towel
'No I'm not!' And off he goes*

Well, *we* were amused.

I know it's not earth-shattering. He just changed his mind; he decided not to be cold.

Let's face it, standing there shivering was a bit boring. (The next part of the story is that he went over and chatted to a group of French girls but that's not relevant here.)

What is relevant here is the quick change. It was unusual. You don't usually change your mind about being cold, do you? You're either cold or you're not. But he simply decided not to be. It was a transformation and we were struck by the sudden ease of it.

We were so struck, in fact, that we've used the term 'do a John on the beach' ever since. We use it when we want to make some change.

In the middle of the night like John on the beach I said, 'No, I'm not. I'm not emotional'. And off I went, unemotional. It may sound glib but it was like that. I did a quick-change turn-around and made a huge difference in an instant.

Last night I turned it around, so I was lying awake but not stressed and not trying to sleep – genuinely. Because it was genuine I fell asleep. I have a lot to do this morning and an early start, but I embraced that last night and the same this morning. I can rest in bed tonight. I'm not going to think about it beyond that.

That's how ditching insomnia gets you to sleep naturally. I allow myself to rest; my body will take care of sleep for me.

I get that lovely sense of freedom. I don't have to be looking for ways of getting to sleep anymore. No more nights suffering worry and frustration or desperately trying to stay calm enough to fall asleep. That's over for good. I know I can do the emotional-to-practical turn-around any time I like. It's like a breath of fresh air.

I have a new mindset: for me insomnia does not exist.

When you get into the mind-switching and feel the transformation you will not be an insomniac anymore.

I think at this point we could do with a ditch-and-switch tabulation (not as painful as it sounds!):

Ditch	Switch
Insomnia	Natural sleep
Try to sleep	Leave it to your body
Desperate to sleep	Being awake doesn't matter
Emotional	Practical
Insomniac	Ex-insomniac

3
Everything's alright

Insomnia-free

I've come a long way. I confronted insomnia and cast all fear of it aside. And now I have come to the position of saying, 'I don't have insomnia anymore. And it's permanent.' I love being able to say that and it being true. It has been quite a journey but such an interesting, worthwhile one. I'm glad I had insomnia, glad it was chronic, glad I struggled and came through.

"I do not have insomnia and I know it is permanent."

Q. How can you be so sure?

A. Because I choose to have that no-doubt mindset

Now I have made myself insomnia-free I will never go back to having it in my life. I am an ex-insomniac. I know it and I make it true; the two go hand in hand. When I say I don't have insomnia anymore, it *is* true. I say to myself: it doesn't matter if I'm awake; being awake is not insomnia; I'll rest and let my body take care of sleep.

I really can believe it when I feel the effect on myself of my own confident words. In the middle of the night, awake, I know I am going to be alright.

I reassure myself with words like: everything's alright, it's fine to be awake. When I speak to myself like that I am harnessing real, powerful emotion. Not sentimental emotion but deeper, more productive than that. I am recognising the responses of the child inside me and addressing them in a rational, practical way. I am a parent comforting a child.

"But is it true? Is everything alright?" the child inside me asks.

"Yes it is. It is true." The parent imparts this truth and knowledge to the child.

When I make things better for myself in this way I am producing that virtuous circle of confidence and control.

I don't mean you're in control of insomnia. As long as insomnia exists you will never control it. I mean you're in control of your mindset: for you insomnia does not exist. You are confident in your new mindset because when you try it out it works.

What about stress?

Q. How do you control things going round in your mind stopping you from sleeping?

A. You switch from emotional to practical and get yourself out of the vicious circle of stress and insomnia.

I'm glad I managed to turn things around to seeing the positive instead of the negative side. That's a great benefit I've derived from struggling with insomnia and finding my way out of it. I did it last night, finding my way out of the feeling of lots of areas of stress converging on me. In the night the thoughts and fears about not sleeping mesh in with the issues and concerns accumulated during the day. And it needs something powerful to turn things around when you're bogged down with it all.

Where can I get this power? Not on the internet or instore. I get it from myself. The power is in mind-switching.

The meeting was a bit unsatisfactory in a way, but the main thing was the way I was able to deal with the feelings. In the past I would have ruminated on it during the night, going over every detail in my head with no chance of getting rid of it, other than it running its own course. But this time I tackled it from the start; I recognised the syndrome (of rumination) and didn't want it/couldn't be bothered with it, so I knocked it on the head as immediately and as thoroughly as I was able to achieve.

My changed mindset on sleep enables me to be practical, so I rest and leave it to my body to decide about sleep.

I had two phases of being awake in the night and got up twice for bathroom and drink of water. The second phase was more prolonged – instead of going straight back to sleep, I lay awake for quite a long time – the actual length of time was irrelevant to me. My attitude was this: I'm not trying to go to sleep (I know that's counter-productive and stopped doing it ages ago). I can't decide to fall asleep – my body will do that when it's ready. I can decide whether I want to stay in bed or get up – that's up to me, depending on how I feel about it. How I feel at the time – nothing to do with how I'm going to feel at some point in the future, or how I may have felt in the past. None of that matters now I don't have insomnia.

Other issues may still be there; they don't go away. But I find the stress response to them disappears when I ditch the stress of insomnia.

No good or bad

Positive language and positive attitude go hand in hand. That's bread and butter to an ex-insomniac, and so different from the negative attitudes and language associated with insomnia. You can really see the difference in people's responses to being awake.

An ex-insomniac might say:

> "It's alright not to be asleep. It's fine to find yourself awake in the night, even if it's for quite a while. You can rest while you're awake and let your body decide about sleep. Basically, being awake isn't a bad thing. There's no pressure."

Martin could be a potential insomniac:

> *I've listened to M saying all kinds of things about his sleeping, which to me now seem counter-productive, against the grain of natural sleep. He talks in terms of good, bad, better, worse nights. He wonders if it's the bed or the room, and what elements might be significant. At night he hopes he'll get a good sleep, and in the morning he assesses it: "Only managed five hours last night". The*

word 'managed' says it all – he's tried and failed. I've been noticing this build-up of negative wording coming from M over the past weeks. I wonder if he's talking himself into insomnia.

I was like that. Negative wording stopped me being able to relax about not sleeping. It gave me a negative attitude, and it kept me looking back, judging the night I'd had.

There's no such thing as a bad night's sleep to an ex-insomniac. Even saying a 'good' night is an unnecessary judgment.

Natural sleep comes from allowing my body to decide if it wants to sleep. I don't need to have an opinion on it at all; no assessments are needed. My body may not want sleep, simple as that. Allow it. I can just rest and relax about being awake. That's all.

I don't even mention sleep these days in my diary. It's not an issue, there's no good or bad, I like sleeping when I do, whenever it is, but I take it for granted (in a nice way). When I'm not sleeping, that's fine too.

Blaming

I used to think my sleep environment and my routine were crucial to whether I slept or not. So everything had to be just right. Now I please myself what I do – I ditch things I used to stick slavishly to. Every item ditched, however small, is a kick in the teeth to insomnia. I like that.

Pandering to insomnia makes you self-conscious of everything you do (and your partner does) around bedtime. And when things have to be right, you end up blaming the person who gets it wrong. You can waste a lot of time and emotional energy on that. When blaming gets tied in with fussing and pressure – details that make the difference between one of you either being able to sleep or having insomnia – the sleep environment becomes a minefield. You get so used to transferring your frustration onto another person, usually the one closest to you, and it becomes a habit.

The more frustrated I was with insomnia, the more I would look for what had triggered it. Often that meant blaming the person who had disturbed me, and the more blaming I did, the more frustrated and angry I became.

M often brings subjects up as he's getting ready for bed – he finds that a good time to discuss things. I used to put the blame for my insomnia on him doing that. I'd think it was selfish and inconsiderate – he knew I needed to read and be quiet. Last night was different; it was me in control, not some vague inevitable insomnia entity. I was on track with the discussion, and that helped M who then helped me. I was awake for a while, then fell asleep. Much better all round.

It helped me relax about being awake when I ditched the blaming. I could just rest.

You have to be able to let the other person off the hook instead of nagging them. You have to switch your perspective. But it's actually very difficult to think: I may not be right. And give another person's standpoint my attention. I'm entrenched in my own position, and the issues around sleep are so personal to me. But making that switch happen is surprisingly liberating. That makes me work at it even more.

At the moment I'm overcoming the feelings associated with being woken up early in the morning, before 6.30, by M making a noise moving his computer out of the bedroom. It's a personal challenge to me to get over it. I have so much history connected with those sleep/being woken up issues. I do very well with it. 'I'll get over it' is my mantra. And I will. I'll go to Pilates this evening, I'll be tired and I'll sleep tonight – but not make it too much of an issue – just a practical strategy to keep me on track.

Get the overview

Last night ruminating hit me unawares.

I woke in the night feeling angry about Emma's criticism and lay there dwelling on it, not fully awake. I'm usually okay now with this sort of thing. I'm used to ditching the troublesome thoughts, not getting stressed by it. But this time I found it hard to shake. And it was so trivial too – what someone said just in passing. Isn't it funny how such small things can be so annoyingly specific to your psyche, and cause trouble way beyond common sense?

It happens all the time; things people say during the day come back to bug me at night. It seems I can't stop my mind going over and over what someone's said or done. Sometimes I need to let myself off the hook. I've done or said something wrong, I've apologised and I'm waiting for the other person to let me off. But they don't. It leaves me going over it in my mind as I lie awake. Okay, feeling bad about what I've done or said helps me to be a sensitive, moral person. It's corrosive, though, if I turn it in on myself – ruminating, feeling awful about it, getting stressed or anxious.

Now I've freed myself from insomnia, I won't put up with this kind of mind clutter: dwelling on things from the past, ruminating about what someone said or did today, lying awake worrying. I have to get rid of the bother of it all. It is essential to find a practical way round the problem. I insist on it for myself. I don't need to waste time and mental energy ruminating. I can turn it around.

When I eventually got up to take some paracetamol I was able to recognise my anger and my ruminating, so I was then halfway to rationalising it. As soon as I started to address Emma's comments as if they were right and could be helpful, my whole physiology changed. That new perspective took away all the negative emotion. It was like magic.

I am an ex-insomniac and I had recognised the need for a mind-switch. From being bogged down inside the stress, I jumped to watching my brain stressing from the outside.

This is what I mean by getting the overview. It's what to do with stress and it's the difference between the vicious and the virtuous circles.

Here's how it worked:

> First, I established I'm not trying to get to sleep; that's important. I used my mantra 'it doesn't matter if I'm awake'.

Next I ditched my emotional response and switched to a practical overview.

I was then able to tackle head-on what I was ruminating about. Basically (with that particular diary example) I changed my view of the comments.

I took on my practical voice and it gave me confidence. The confidence gave me control of my mindset. And so on.

This is the virtuous circle of confidence and control.

As I do more and more of this kind of ditching and switching, my ex-insomniac mindset will be taking root and growing.

4
Being awake

Review of a sleepless night

Time is a massive issue to insomniacs. To their minds, time awake in the night is endless and scary, an alien thing outside their control.

But as an ex-insomniac I embrace time in the night. I am not afraid of it because now I have made it my own. It's up to me what I do with the time and, if I don't want to, I needn't take any notice of it at all.

It's 3pm. I've decided to write this review of the sleepless night I had last night, which I haven't had for quite some time:

Don't wait for sleep. Simply observe you're awake. Don't be disappointed. Remember sleep is up to your body and resting is fine.

It's your choice how you spend the awake time, and it doesn't matter where you are/what you're doing/what time it is. You can look at the time if you want (or not) but it's not an issue.

One's natural instinct is to find it scary, being awake when you expect to be asleep. 'Keep the faith'. It really doesn't matter – you'll be alright. Nothing bad will happen to you.

I don't think I slept at all, but I probably did. I could remember some images from a dream-like trance, a form of sleep, and enough to satisfy my body's needs.

Don't try to think why you're not sleeping e.g. caffeine, over-stimulating conversation, stressed about... The list will be endless and pointless. So don't bother. It's easier to think, 'Who cares? So what? A lot less fuss and trouble and, as you don't have insomnia, it's irrelevant, N/A

Remember you have ditched insomnia and ditched things stay ditched. Being awake is not insomnia.

You may feel rough the next day – 'spaced out' is how I described it to myself. But you're not ill.

You'll survive. Have a rest when you can – no need to stay awake on purpose so you'll be tired at bedtime.

When you next get to bed, rest and leave sleep to your body.

When I look at a sleepless night in this factual kind of way, I am a confident ex-insomniac relying on my own mindset. I am in control, using my own resources. How different from looking back in an emotional state, regretting the lost sleep, frustrated and angry, worried about the day ahead!

A sleepless night is a practice session. I use it to my advantage because I treat it as an opportunity for taking control.

Now I'm positive about the 3 hours' sleep and I'll rest as and when I get the chance and I want to, or wait till tonight, if I prefer. It makes no difference, it doesn't matter. I don't have to think about catching up on sleep. I leave it to my body to decide about that.

I like monitoring myself when I'm awake in the night. I see how I'm handling things, and that informs the next time.

Being in the moment

I may be awake when everyone else is asleep, but I am not lonely. I don't watch the clock, as insomniacs do. Instead, I appreciate the present moment. When I relax into my time in the night, I am by myself, relying on my own company.

How different being in the moment is from waiting to go to sleep or trying to sleep and worrying how long it's taking! Now I can look forward to whatever the night brings. I am no longer trapped in the vicious circle of stress and insomnia. I am empowered by the positive circle of confidence and control. And that continues when I get up and start the day.

It worked out fine with the sleep situation. I'm only writing about it for research purposes – otherwise I'd ignore it and move on. Actually that's just what I did yesterday, got on with the day. My attitude to it was the prime factor. As soon as I can, forget the night and only look ahead or at the present, not back. Look ahead in a general way – know I'll be fine, know when I have a sleep opportunity next if my body wants to catch up. And be in the present – enjoy breakfast – allow myself to come round, allow the normality to be there – it will emerge if I don't prevent it by looking back negatively, perceiving a problem. I put a Roy Orbison/Otis Redding compilation on as I drove to my appointment and allowed myself to relax, just being – no more than that.

It must have been a year after my switch from insomniac to ex-insomniac – a year's worth of practising with my new mindset – that a lovely event occurred. Our twin granddaughters were born. They inspired me to write poetry and to welcome spending time with them in the night, as I described in my diary:

I thought one of the babies was going to have a disturbed night, but I managed to settle her down and she slept all through after that. It really helps me that I've been through all that insomnia, and nothing fazes me now to do with being kept awake like that. I am perfectly relaxed with it, no worry about when I might get to bed myself. It's a good position to be in.

I could look confidently at my past insomnia and see it as an asset.

I don't mind having things to do. I take on whatever the day and evening bring, knowing now that the sleep will take care of itself. I don't think about it, and I embrace the waking hours during the day, welcoming whatever activities precede going to bed. I've stopped taking it into account, so I don't worry about needing to read till I fall asleep, or being woken up, etc. A lot of that is due to the twins and being up in the night with them, and not minding at all, but actually loving the fact that I'm used to it. It's a kind of extra skill I've acquired, and I feel lucky to have it.

It's a very personal thing. Sometimes, for me, being in the moment has a meditation feel to it. Or my mood may be totally practical. But whatever form the feeling takes, the difference in my situation is so remarkable that I can absolutely bask in it.

Insomnia has always been at the centre of any issues I'm struggling with. I've come so far with that. It's been a long struggle, but now I feel I've come out the other end. For me, it's all connected with being up in the night with the twins; with going so far down with insomnia and still surviving; not only that but striving more and more to be in control. I feel I've been on a long journey and can now rest from it – that feeling came to me after I'd been with the babies all night – it was more spiritual than mental in the end – a beautiful feeling of sereneness within myself.

Sleep is not an issue

Before I reached the turning-point, I had been living and working with chronic insomnia. I had left teaching because of it. It had become impossible to carry on in the structured routine of school life while coping with the stress of not sleeping.

Over time we had built up a small business letting properties. We started with one flat in Brighton and moved on to owning houses which we let out as rooms in house shares. I went on, after teaching, to work full-time managing them. It was hard work especially with the insomnia constantly threatening.

But after the turning-point, I was living and working with my evolving ex-insomniac mindset. What a difference I can tell you! No comparison.

But I *can* compare. I told you how I trawled heroically through my diary notebooks. I have the pages right here and I think they will be illuminating. The benefits kept cropping up all over the place.

I found this example – on holiday in Tobago.

Always strange and disorienting when you arrive in a foreign, alien environment. That's how it seems at first, especially when there's a time difference (5 hours) and your body clock needs to adjust, as well as your mind. For me, the fact that I don't have insomnia anymore is really helpful. Since sleeping is of little to no significance, this is not an issue at all. I had a full night's sleep, waking up at what would have been 7.30am (here 2.30 am), then back to sleep till 5.30am when we got up to unpack before breakfast, which started at 7am. It's so humid here and no air conditioning in the restaurant – all open but makes no difference unless you're sitting right under a fan – must ensure that next time if we can. It's all part of getting used to it, getting your bearings. Same as at home – take things as they come, stay with the moment and gradually relax into it all.

In the end insomnia has made me stronger. I find I'm on the look-out for benefits in all different situations. The possibilities are endless. And they are all entirely up to me.

Before, the insomnia fed off the stress, and the stress fed off the insomnia. Not anymore. I made a chink in that vicious circle. Now, being in control gives me confidence, and confidence helps me be in control. I have created a brand-new virtuous circle. That's really empowering.

I had stopped defining myself as an insomniac. I no longer

felt sorry for myself or regarded myself as ill. I became far too matter-of-fact for that.

The circumstances were so familiar to me – the things that would have led to insomnia in the past: alarm set for 6 am, the packing to finish, travel arrangements to check, not sure I've given myself time to prepare and plan ahead, will I cope without sleep? It was pressures like these that gave me insomnia originally, but not anymore. I don't mind being awake now. I accept it. I knew, even if I didn't sleep, none of that stuff would stress me.

They were not pressures anymore; they were just circumstances. It works a treat – a change of name to ex-insomniac and a change of attitude all in one simplified package. The difference is astounding.

What about setbacks?

Insomnia is not part of my life now and I will never go back to it.

Q. Sounds great, but aren't you setting yourself up for disappointment? What if the insomnia returns?

Unfortunately I didn't sleep last night – wondered if the coffee was not decaf, but it's probably not helpful to look for reasons. I don't want to feel disappointed either – just put it behind me and don't think too much about it. Don't make an issue out of it. I was quite good about it during the night, not allowing myself to get bogged down. I said to myself I would deal with the day ahead as it came – no need to worry about it in advance. Nothing to be frightened of – it works. It's about trusting myself to deal with the future when it comes, not rehearse it beforehand.

And the next day:

Back home – long, long sleep last night, following sleep during the evening too, so well rested now. I still don't count the night without sleep as insomnia, because of my attitude to it. It did not worry me at the time, as I knew I would be okay whatever.

I used to regard a sleepless night as a setback. I'd been feeling really pleased with my progress, and then I'd find myself awake all night. I couldn't help but feel disappointed.

But now I have a secret weapon; I am armed with the name ex-insomniac and the mindset to go with it. I can use them to change my attitude to a sleepless night. To my mind now, it's not scary or harmful to be awake for hours. Even if I have a big day ahead of me and have to get up early, I can embrace the time awake.

In fact, I could have a new name for setback. How about calling it research opportunity? A sleepless night becomes useful to me for feedback. "How am I doing? This will be good practice for me. See if my ideas are working."

So disappointment doesn't come into it at all. Disappointment has been ditched along with insomnia.

A. The question 'what if the insomnia returns?' is meaningless when you are an ex-insomniac.

Part Two
Growing the mindset

I had to leave teaching because of insomnia. What if I'd known then that insomnia could be ditched?

My ex-insomniac approach would have helped me not only with sleeping but also with the demanding and challenging job.

It's about a mindset that's good for sleep, flowing naturally into a mindset that's good for work.

Part Two is about practising the Insomnia Ditch-and-Switch and seeing how it progresses.

5

A product that works

The insomnia ditch-and-switch

The stress of teaching while I had insomnia eventually overtook me and I was forced to leave my job.

How would I find teaching now after a sleepless night – not how it was back then, but as an ex-insomniac?

It would have been great.

In the night I could have allowed my body to deal with sleep – no need for me to bother about it at all. What bliss! That would have given me a relaxed attitude to the day ahead, whether I had slept or not. If I hadn't slept, I'd know I could rest in bed next time and leave sleep to my body. It would have helped me to enjoy the moment, be involved in each activity I'd planned for my class. Yes I would have appreciated the creativity of teaching even more.

Q. What about the stresses of the job?

A. They are there whatever. You deal with those as a teacher. You don't want them bound up with the vicious circle of stress and insomnia – that's not to be recommended!

A PRODUCT THAT WORKS

Gradually the stressful picture of teaching with insomnia faded and I realised after a while I was missing being creative. I was looking for something extra, something creative to do. And it was under my nose all along. How interesting that tackling insomnia became a creative project! The project is the ex-insomniac mindset and the writing of this book about it.

I was still suffering from insomnia when I discovered the Rottingdean Writers' Group and decided to join. My first assignment was to write a poem based on a photograph. (I've included it in End notes 1.) I hadn't written a poem since I was at primary school but I loved having a go at it. And it wasn't long after that I started writing my diary.

I chose to start my book – my memoir – with the *'horrible horrible night'* diary entry. I was at rock bottom. My so-called solutions were sucking me further into the insomnia trap. This was a plea for help: *Why can't the results be permanent?*

The dire situation created the need for something new and different.

And then I had my eureka-moment lightbulb flash. A product started to break through. It was the insomnia ditch-and-switch™. How glad I am that I invented it!

Notes on my invention:

Frustration and tedium came first, exasperation with the received wisdom and its products. There must be a better way.

Then came the breakthrough. The big idea: ditch insomnia itself.

It had to be tested to see if the big idea worked in practice.

So my eureka moment was followed by perseverance: with testing and feedback.

The task: make it into a product that works – reliably and consistently: first for myself, then for anyone else. Bear in mind, for example, people who have to get up for work in the morning and do a demanding job – think back to how it was for me that time in Kemptown.

Does this ex-insomniac mindset (not having insomnia permanently) work, and if it does how does it keep working and for anybody, for every person with insomnia i.e. universal?

As I compiled the book from diary entries, notes and pieces of writing, I repeatedly asked myself this question: Does this work as a product for the reader?

Theory is a start, but the hard bit is finding out how it can work in practice. It was not theoretical actually. No, this eureka moment was practical from the start. It was a balance of do and think, gut feeling and thought-out 'does this work?' and, if it does, how exactly does it keep working in situ – in bed awake in the night.

I was doing well, putting theory into practice, giving myself feedback about being awake – a process of trial and error.

This turned out to be a refining and encapsulating process with the insomnia ditch-and-switch emerging as a product.

The mindset I switched to had this key element: leave sleep to my body. That's how I ditched insomnia itself.

Questions to the inventor

Q. How do you test out the new mindset in situ?

A. Awake in the night you ask yourself: what works? Try leaving sleep to your body. Your role is to rest. Test out the new mindset by using mantras: leave sleep to my body; I don't have insomnia; it doesn't matter if I'm awake.

You might have a lightbulb moment. Aha, letting go is taking control! You've let go of trying to sleep, waiting for sleep, worrying about being awake. You've ditched insomnia and you switch – you rest and leave sleep to your body.

Practise over and over. Use mantras to encapsulate your new mindset. Have faith that a small significant thing repeated will change the big picture. Give yourself feedback.

Q. What if I still have a sleepless night?

A. Learn from what doesn't work – setbacks are useful.

Perhaps you didn't let go of trying to sleep last night. You couldn't let go of worrying. It doesn't mean the new mindset hasn't worked. You can let go tonight. It's trial and error. Make mistakes. Recognise unhelpful thinking.

Q. Can you give examples of error, mistake, unhelpful thinking in this context?

A. Yes, they will be mindset mistakes.

Did I change my mindset last night and ditch insomnia? Did I switch to allowing my body to deal with sleep? Maybe I didn't let myself go enough to do that.

Q. But it's not always like that, not always possible. What do I do then?

A. You know when it's possible to do a ditch-and-switch. You know when suffering is in your mind, when it could be an error of mindset, an attitude problem. Of course you can stay with the suffering – it's a choice. Keep on suffering with insomnia. Maybe you held onto your insomnia last night. What stage are you at? What exactly were you holding onto last night: piled-on stress? A downward spiral? Mind-numbing boredom? Tonight you can decide not to have insomnia. Ditch it. You have the need to make a change. Switch. Allow the change. Make it quick and effective.

Do a small thing in situ every night and the big picture will change too without you planning it.

Balance of think and do

I choose my own mindset. The human brain has the capacity to watch itself (and watch itself watching itself!). This surely makes me the world expert on myself. I conduct research appropriate to my expertise. I study myself, test out my ideas and give myself feedback.

I can affect my conscious mind directly and positively. And the nice thing is there's a lot going on behind the scenes in my mind too. There may be breakthroughs which are conscious, and some effects will be unconscious ones.

It's a good feeling – being in charge of my own life. I switch to my practical mode of thinking and the more practice I get the more confidence I build up.

I feel myself to be more and more in control – that comes from trusting myself and being confident about my own feelings and thinking. I look to identify what is working for me, because I alone can sense what is right for me.

Q. How does studying myself help with natural sleep?

You're right to wonder. I said natural sleep meant leaving it to my body, so I need to get my head out of it and let go. Then I said to get my head into it and take control. How can I best explain this apparent contradiction? Maybe a table:

Studying myself	Natural sleep
Theory	Practice
Think	Do
Head in	Head out
Intervene	Do nothing

| Take control | Let go of control |
| Insomnia ditch-and-switch | Leave sleep to my body |

These are not contradictory. You can see they all fit together.

A. Studying myself helps me to adjust or alter my attitudes, in such a way that I move away from insomnia and towards natural sleep.

I allow my body to decide about sleep, and it's simple. It feels natural. But I've built up years of stopping my body from doing what it can and wants to do – years of resisting, worrying, rehearsing disaster, and so on. It's quite a process dismantling this structure, but the results are more and more astounding. Letting go feels marvellous. But sometimes I have to take control, when my emotions have taken over, to get my practical voice.

When I take out the emotion, my head is helping my body, allowing it to do what it does naturally. Head and body work best together, not one fighting against the other.

When we'd finished talking over the Bonchurch plan, M got up (6am) with no prospect of more sleep, he said. I settled back to see if my body wanted more sleep. To do that, I rested; that was my role. Not trying to sleep – just resting is enough. Actually I did sleep some more. I had an early start and nearly overslept. That's natural sleep, not forced (which is impossible), not waited for, not focused on.

I ditched insomnia permanently by switching my mindset on

being awake. My head reminds me that I'm not trying to sleep. Then I get my head out of it and leave sleep to my body. After a while I take sleep for granted and don't think about it at all.

Tackling insomnia myself

It is perfectly reasonable to regard psychologists as the experts and to think it is they, not us, who hold the knowledge about the mind. Generally we know there are psychologists, psychiatrists and therapists out there, and we hope they will be able to cure us if the need arises. You may not have given it much thought. Mostly in our everyday lives we don't think about our mind. But it's when something like sleep issues crop up that we are compelled to wonder about what's going on inside the brain. We seek answers and we want to know who can give us those answers.

Then there's the popular science we read in magazines and on internet sites informing us about sleep issues. The language used by people offering cures is geared to showing how much you need their cure for insomnia. Here's a selection from a typical magazine article: damage to health, sleep disruptors, proven system, follow instructions, sleep cycle, brainwaves and phases of sleep, monitored by scientists using an electroencephalogram, sleeping environment, sleep disorder.

Putting your faith in a particular method creates a type of desperation: "What if it doesn't work, even when I've had complete faith and followed all instructions religiously? It means I'm a hopeless case. There's something wrong with me, some failing that other people don't have. This failing is probably innate, so I'm incurable. My condition is obviously worse, my case more severe than others". People who are at the desperate stage have to believe there are experts with the knowledge to cure. If you are an insomniac, your mission is to find a cure.

But of course, if I don't have insomnia anymore and never will again, I don't need a cure. This simple statement gives me freedom. I am no longer dependent on anyone else. And no one exists who could cure me of insomnia anyway. There is no fixed and definitive body of knowledge about psychology, and there is no one who has the answers about what is going on in my mind.

Q. But what about underlying causes of my insomnia?

A. My point is that, if I tackle the insomnia, there's no need to try delving into what's at the root of it. I went through that process with the psychotherapist and it only caused more stress. My mother really wasn't in any way to blame. Poor Mum! The therapist apologised in the end, but there was no need – it was all interesting.

As an ex-insomniac I deal with stress as it crops up, and any hidden stress is helped along the way. It will all be productive because I'm on a confidence-and-control trajectory. (Do you like that different wording for a virtuous circle?) I'm then indirectly affecting my unconscious mind, sorting underlying issues. It's an excellent package deal.

I tackled insomnia myself. I used the ditch-and-switch to get out of the vicious circle I was in. And now I keep practising. Sometimes I'm taking control and at other times letting go of control. This means studying myself, being practical and building trust in myself.

I got a bit bogged down last night – something about the half-asleep mode that fosters rumination. It was to do with my performance at the open mic – only a minor slip-up when I was reading out my Canal Trip poem – but it created a slight mood change and turned into that annoying ruminating. As soon as I was fully awake this morning, I got my practical overview of it and had a plan immediately for the next Baltica (I'll read just one longer poem, Grytviken). I'm glad I can do that mind-switching, and I think it gets easier with practice.

Q. But won't studying yourself make you self-conscious? Surely that's a bad thing where sleep is concerned.

A. Studying myself doesn't make me self-conscious. One is so different from the other, they are almost opposites. I'll set it out as a table to show you what I mean:

Studying yourself	Being self-conscious
Towards natural sleep	Towards insomnia
Relaxing	Stressful
On purpose	Unwanted
Expansive	Restricting

I study myself on purpose. It allows me to gain feedback for tackling any situation or issue affecting me. It's an amazing tool. It leads me towards natural sleep, because I can jump from being at the mercy of my emotions to taking charge of them. I use my own strategies to deal with stress in the night – my mantras help me with this. And the same strategies work just as well during the day.

Self-consciousness is unwanted. It happens to me. It's when the situation controls me, not me taking control of the situation. When I had insomnia I was self-conscious about sleep. I was trying too hard. I ditched all that, so it didn't matter if I was awake and I let my body decide about sleep.

It's up to me what I call this self-study thing. I might prefer: a practical approach to living, giving myself feedback, having self-awareness, developing my relationship with myself. Like mantras, I choose the wording that works for me.

Author's note: In fact, do you find the word 'mantra' useful? You don't have to call it a mantra if the connotations put you off. Words and concepts (and how you use them) are very much connected with your own individual take on it all.

6
Practising the mindset

Relaxed and simple

I found a relaxed mindset on sleeping gave me a relaxed approach to the day ahead.

It's so interesting how attitudes I have in the night time influence how I deal with the daytime – and vice versa. I change my perspective on insomnia and, as it changes, my perspective on other areas of life changes too.

A nice full day coming today: massage this morning, back lunchtime for snack, shower and wash hair, before meeting J at 3pm for the snooker/Pilates session, back here with J for dinner and out to writers' group for 7.30 start. It's all good stuff. The timing, dinner, etc. has all been planned, so no need to race ahead in my thoughts. It's an example of enjoying each part as it comes and not spoiling it by thinking of the next part and the one after that. I know I have a tendency to do that – or used to. I'm much better now at enjoying the present, getting the most out of each thing I'm doing, rather than seeing it only in the context of a planned sequence. I suppose that was tied in with not wanting to make mistakes, wanting everything to run smoothly and to rehearse the plan in my head in order for that to happen. I can see that tendency clearly now, and I don't like it – it spoils things because I don't appreciate them.

Going over plans in my head in a ruminating way is counter-productive. That kind of rehearsal is worry. Planning should be a more useful kind of rehearsal – it has to be practical. If rehearsing my plans turns into emotional 'what-ifs', it tips into stress. Moving towards the natural and simple means giving plans their own place, allowing me to enjoy the moment.

It's about getting the balance between intervening and allowing, between taking control and letting go of control. I'm getting a feel for which is appropriate and when.

I might need to rationalise what I'm stressing about in the night and maybe work out a plan of action. Or it may be a case of doing nothing, except perhaps a John-on-the-beach to break away from the emotion. What seemed complicated could just turn out to be simple.

In the night I was in the grip of thoughts and feelings that were hard to control. I had to make a real effort to rationalise my ruminating, using strategies and mantras. My childish psyche had to be stopped in its tracks. When I woke up in the morning, the content had ceased to be important, and I didn't need to take action to put it right. The issue was really a non-issue. That was my feedback – simple.

Non-judgmental criticism

As an ex-insomniac I appreciate how giving myself feedback really works. After a sleepless night. I look back and review how I handled it in a factual, non-emotional way. I learn from what worked and what didn't work. Trial and error. For future reference.

It's about getting an overview of the situation and cutting through the waste-of-time worry thinking. This self-critique is the kind of approach that simplifies. It's a creative way of going about things, part of my ex-insomniac mindset – I feel I am working towards living my life creatively and practically.

Self-critique has become a part of my relationship with myself. It provides me with valuable self-knowledge and is totally different from being critical in a self-diminishing way.

Here's an example, a potentially frustrating episode:

Maria was ready to complain at me as I walked in. I dissipated her criticism but the episode has left me emotionally stirred up. I need to look at that within myself – then it will all be useful to me. The only part of the interaction which concerns me is the practical issue of getting the Anthology out and ready for the Fair. But I can use my own reactions to give myself feedback. I need to take on the criticisms I bristle at, and look at them as unemotionally as I can. It will be interesting but not easy, I know.

Being criticised can be disheartening. Nobody likes to be criticised. Why would you? But it's a fact of life. People judge. It's human nature. It's how our brains try to make sense of the world, by categorising and labelling. We are all givers and receivers of judgments. But it should be possible to deal with this criticism thing in a practical way. I'm sure that receiving criticism can even be empowering. It depends on how it's taken. If I take it personally, I turn it in on myself. Alternatively, I can use it in some way to make it helpful.

Being overly critical of myself is no use at all; nor is trying all the time to assess myself positively. Critiquing myself involves a balance of praise and criticism, giving myself credit when it's due and, where appropriate and useful, criticising myself in a non-judgmental way. It depends on how I look at it – useful self-study that moves me forward or self-defeating confirmation of failure. I would never go back to that negative mindset, now I've experienced the helpful, practical feedback I give myself as an ex-insomniac.

Trust myself

I don't have insomnia anymore – haven't for quite some time – and yet I still use the basics all the time. The original strategy went like this:

> In the middle of the night I was brave and did a turn-around. I switched from emotional to practical, getting an overview of myself in the situation instead of getting bogged down in it. I was in control – so I could let go. I rested and let my body decide about sleep.
>
> My mind and my body were working together in a natural way – a wonderful, liberating connection.

I use that mind-body link all the time now to help me with the stresses of day-to-day living. It helps me get a positive mental attitude to how I'm feeling.

Q. But where do you begin when you're feeling really down?

I know what you mean – sometimes my mood can be so low that the very last thing I'm feeling is confident and ready to turn things around.

A. I begin by confirming my trust in myself.

Have confidence that I will move from emotional to practical. It may be over a period of time or I may feel like doing a John-on-the-beach.

It's up to me, because I'm in charge of my own mindset. Be patient with myself, if that applies. Or tell myself off, if that seems more appropriate. I may want to allow myself some anger, self-pity even. If that feels right, give it a whirl, let it all out. Observe it. Then do a shift, if I can at that point, or wait.

Sometimes I use the same strategies I used for dealing with stress in the night. I give myself feedback on how I'm doing. Do I have a mantra that would be good for this present situation? That's if I feel it would work to give myself a bit of a kick. Don't wallow in self-pity, for example! Or a kinder one: be patient, have faith. That would be allowing my mood to come right in its own good time.

At other times I really can't improve my mood directly by rationalising and problem solving. But then something will take me out of myself when I'm not thinking about it.

It's interesting what can lift your mood. I was very heavy in the afternoon and couldn't shake it before the writers' group. (I'd fallen asleep, instead of going out for a walk as I'd intended, and woke up feeling groggy and in need of fresh air.) I made sure I said only positive things about everyone's writing this time. In my own mind I made up for my controversial comments last time. That must have helped my mood because I found the evening really enjoyable.

And then there's tiredness. Even experienced ex-insomniacs can misinterpret tiredness as stress. Because I'm feeling really tired, my brain might mislead me into thinking I'm stressed. Tiredness and stress are easily confused.

I could just be thinking: "I'm really tired, so I'll have an early night resting and reading my book in bed." That would be harmless and cosy. But instead I'm linking it with a specific source of potential stress and assuming that's the cause of my tiredness. It makes me have panicky, anxious thoughts. "That's what's stopping me sleeping and making me feel terrible."

My unconscious mind does that. It's trying to do me a favour – linking up these stressors for me; showing me that one is the cause of the other. It's trying to bring order. Completely random thoughts would be chaotic. However, the link may be false this time, misleading.

But knowing this can happen – that I am being misled – means I can intervene to prevent it. I need to prevent it because it can be quite a corrosive process. Unless I do something it will continue to affect me. The link has been made. It's obvious so it's irrevocable. I can be physically tired from bodily exertion and then – what a shame! – mix it all up with mental stuff.

That's the familiar vicious circle I had with stress and insomnia, which of course I'm not going to re-enter. I'm an ex-insomniac. I have the confidence and trust in myself to recognise all that and ditch it. Turn the situation around from emotional to practical. Get the overview. Each time I do this I'm confirming how well it works, adding to my experience, and strengthening my mind and body confidence.

Good, the poetry group is starting again – that will be a great way to be in the moment. It's what I need to slow things down when there's such a lot going on. I don't feel as relaxed with things as I'd like to be. It's probably tiredness underlying – so I shouldn't extrapolate from that to thinking it's down to M or something in me. Just like I dealt with insomnia, don't look for causes and triggers. It's good advice. Just go along, not racing ahead, not over-analysing (and probably drawing false conclusions anyway), enjoying the moment within each day. Relaxing and resting as and when I can.

So I'm practising my ex-insomniac approach – doing a ditch-and-switch in the sleep situation, and then carrying the emotional to practical mind-switch over into other parts of my life.

Other parts of my life, like having a domestic argument, for example. That's life, it's not just children that get into squabbles. A typical quote: "I'm feeling terrible now. S/he's to blame for how I feel. It's all because of the hurtful thing s/he just said. I'd be fine otherwise."

But I'm probably wrong. I can't tell exactly what's made me upset and angry. In an argument we think we remember every detail faithfully. But it's deceptive, because the memory part of our brain is really inaccurate, even regarding what's just been said. There are all sorts of messages going through the brain to influence and distort our perception.

Like insomnia, don't bother looking for causes and triggers – who said this or who did that. It doesn't get us very far. Much better to deal with changing the mood and moving forward, rather than looking back and blaming. As an ex-insomniac I know just how unhelpful that kind of blaming mindset can be. But if I can get the feel of it – not easy in the midst of an argument – I can do a John-on the-beach and make a jump from the vicious circle to the other sort, the one that has a way forward.

I realised it would take one of us to drop the defensive first. "Do you want a cup of tea?" was my strategy. It wasn't as twee as it sounds. Throwing that line in slightly but significantly altered the atmosphere and took us out of it. I got the overview while I was putting the kettle on. I felt pleased with myself because I was using the ex-insomniac mindset. My bitterness fell away pretty much instantly. Emotional had been replaced with practical. The vicious circle made way for the virtuous circle to begin its course.

It's human nature, when arguing, to revert to the usual patterns, the polarised, every-man-for-himself type. They are comfortable in a way, familiar. Finding fault is so easy and oh-so tempting. It's much easier to see things that need changing in others, easier than seeing faults in myself. But seeing relationship issues in terms of faults is not helpful. If I think of it more as being tolerant and working around issues, it can lead to me to seeing things about myself I may want to work on or things to be more flexible about.

Gradually, as with insomnia, negative patterns can be replaced by the feel-good, positive type. I'm used to ditching and switching now. I know I have to go through the negative stuff first and trust myself to find the patience and confidence to instigate a change. Then the virtuous circle gathers momentum and each person's self-belief has a chance to expand.

Cherry pick

As an ex-insomniac I'll find my own way forward. It's really about taking whatever fits in with my way of thinking and making it my own. I call it cherry picking.

I don't always know or realise straight away what ideas could be of use to me. But I'm on the alert, recognising what I'm ready for. It's being open to hearing or seeing what makes sense to me and what relates to me. Take it, whole or part, and make it my own. Tailor it to myself. Observe, tune in. I know what's right for me and, armed with my ex-insomniac skills, I have the independence and confidence to know if I want to take on someone else's set of ideas. (Unlike an insomniac who, needing to believe in experts and cures, comes to rely on them.)

I make my own connections and get my own angle. I choose my own mantras. They are my aides-mémoire, so I can easily get back on track. A short-hand way of remembering how to move forward. I used mantras when I was struggling and continue to use them now in any situation.

Author's note: See if any part of my experience resonates with you/feels right for you now. Or leave it till later and come back to it. Everyone is different – it's all about personal choice.

I find my own personal truth from knowledge I have made

my own. If I add on to my own individual expertise the knowledge I have chosen to acquire from someone else, then I have a powerful combination.

Now I use sources such as newspaper and magazine articles for indirect help and motivation i.e. how not to think, what attitudes not to have. I recognise immediately any counter-productive language and advice, be it scientific or anecdotal. They mostly pile on the pressure. In effect, it goes like this: you must sleep, or beware the direst of consequences, but it's really important to relax about it or you won't sleep.

Have that pinch of salt always at the ready. I don't really need it, though. I know myself how to react to sleeping and not sleeping. I don't need to be told how I should view it. But if I want to take on advice which seems good to me, that's different. It's great to be open to ideas, and I sense which ones are right for me.

I used to take on advice I'd been reading about not having naps during the day. This only seemed important when I had insomnia. Now I don't have it, it's up to me when I fall asleep. I don't even think about how it might affect my sleep at night. It seems irrelevant to me. What freedom!

I can even cherry pick from my own thoughts and ideas. I'm like another person assessing what to take on board, what to reject or adapt, and what I might want to change about myself.

Q. Change myself? I'm not sure I can, and I'm not sure I want to.

A. It's up to you what you want to change, if anything.

But then, maybe 'change' is not a helpful word in this context.

Instead of 'changing myself', better wording might be: discovering or learning about my relationship with myself. When I discover something about myself, it sets in motion a liberating thinking process. And it's completely up to me what I want to learn about, tackle or alter.

I can cherry pick from my own thinking and decide what, if anything, I want to give attention to. If there's a crisis in my life or some issue like insomnia, I may well want to make changes related to myself. If in my own perception it's a negative thing affecting my life, I may want to tackle my mindset. But I can't analyse my mind directly at the time (impossible for anyone). I can deal with my own reactions though. I can have an effect on my own feeling and thinking, even though sometimes it seems like my mind is an impossible tangle of conflicts.

I can work towards a practical problem-solving mindset. I start by trusting myself that I will not be at the mercy of my emotions.

Chairing went well at RW – felt like a successful meeting, everyone read and there was lively critique, as we can rely on with this current group. Rick was back from Botswana, which I'll mention in my follow-up email. I was fine in myself while I was chairing (I just wish people would be a little more admiring of the piece and how it came about, rather than just the editing detail. The creativity gets lost in opinions on the detail.), but I did go into myself afterwards – wanted to get away by myself when others were still there chatting. I found that part quite difficult, as

I just wasn't my usual chatty self. I don't like feeling like that. But I can trust myself that I will come out of it – just allow my body to find its own level – not rush it, trying to think it all out. I'm feeling different this morning and will allow my body – including my unconscious mind – to level out, settle gradually.

7
Ex-insomniac skills

Finding the balance

Jackie and I went off to bed at midnight and left the boys up playing music and drinking even more wine. (M's surprised he feels wrecked this morning.) I was so glad I don't have insomnia anymore, and it's all tied in with attitude during the day and evening. Attitudes to waking hours/sleeping are inter-dependent. It's a balance between enjoying the moment – not worrying about the morning – and thinking ahead, projecting myself into how I want to feel later. For me, it's that balance which is crucial.

Now I've got this idea of balance, I find I'm using it all the time. It helps me to be more relaxed in my waking hours, and that feels good. I can use it, for example, on feelings of frustration.

A bit frustrated – text from J wanting RWG email addresses – so the agenda hasn't been sent after all, in spite of my reminders during his day off yesterday. Why does it frustrate me? I think it's about wanting to have control over the format of the meetings – make sure it continues to be done properly in the way Jen and I thought was best for the new group. But, thinking about it, it has to be sustainable without my input. If I let it run itself, the format will evolve its own way with the current members. No need to be frustrated – let it take its own course with my input as and when required in a relaxed way. Chill out and let go of responsibility for others – it's not my job. Get the balance between input and standing back.

I can use balance to give myself alternatives. I find this helps me to deal with feelings of stress. What is the alternative to ruminating about something? I think it's finding that particular situation interesting. They are two sides of the same coin:

> Dwelling on something in an inward-looking way, going nowhere
>
> Looking at something in a practical way, seeing opportunities

All that's needed is a flip-over of the coin.

It's about observing myself in my present situation and making my own assessment of how I'm doing. It was like that in the sleep situation when I ditched the emotional and switched to the practical. I tuned in and sensed the potential for a different perspective. I looked at the other side of the coin.

It's useful to see the balance between these two sides of the same coin:

> Being in the moment positively
>
> Getting bogged down in the moment

If I tune in and get the practical overview of where I am, I can appreciate the present instead of being swamped by my own fussing. I stopped myself getting bogged down when I ditched the things I used to fuss over in my sleep environment. I made choices between what mattered and what didn't matter. I knew these two sides of the coin were important:

> To be bothered in terms of motivation
>
> Not to be bothered with insignificant choices

I saw the balance and used it to make the situation simple and relaxed. It worked when I ditched insomnia and, once I'd got into it, I realised how useful it could be.

Thoughts while in Harpenden, written in a café:

I didn't let Z's disrupted sleep stress me. I didn't know exactly how or when I would get some extra sleep, but I could play it by ear. Later on in the day I had a nap when the opportunity arose. This is where being in control means having choices. But freedom can also mean not having choices. To stop being an insomniac I had to take my own options away, so I could stop fussing at bedtime. Choice can be stressful. I took away Z's stress this morning – when I was getting her ready to go to Nursery – by not giving her any choice over what to wear. Sometimes it's nice for her to choose, but this time it resulted in one of those toddler tantrums. I thought, "Poor Z, having to do all that fussing over a pair of trousers".

I had to get the overview for her, stop her being stuck in the moment. I knew from my own experience of these things that I had to sort what matters from what doesn't matter. In the moment I can be focusing on unhelpful things. I must find the balance, being in the moment and getting a practical overview.

It's tricky getting the balance – forward planning but not racing ahead in my thoughts. I'm doing quite well though. Being aware of the need for that balance is the secret. It is for me anyway. It makes a day like yesterday much more pleasurable when I take my time to focus on each thing: on the massage/talking to Jane, on the snooker session with J, on the Rottingdean Writers meeting. And looking back there were lots of times when I wasn't thinking anything, just enjoying myself. It was a really full, interesting day.

Tyranny of time

I really want to do what I said and slow things down so I'm in the moment, not racing ahead, consulting my today list. Just thought back to the extreme of that in Peacehaven after J was born – walking along pushing the pram and looking ahead in my pocket diary to see when Spring was coming with its lighter evenings, looking at the extra minutes of daylight. It's a powerful image and symbolism. Obviously I have that tendency (racing ahead – the today list), so it's important to resist the tyranny by getting the balance, as I'm doing now, quite well, I think.

Windy Peacehaven on the cliff top along the coast from Brighton was where we lived when our younger son (of John-on-the-beach fame) was born.

It's interesting to remember that time and compare myself now to what I was like then. I have skills now I didn't have then. Like finding balance in a situation. A balanced mindset. It shows how far I've come.

I wrote this piece for the writers' group. It's a true story. At the time of writing I wanted to fictionalise it and changed my baby to a girl I named Natalie. The title is *Back Home:*

"Go home and bake a cake," the health visitor said to me in the middle of the waiting room, loads of people listening. So here goes. Recipe for a sponge cake, step1: don't put the next foot in front of the other. Step one, then, is impossible; I have to keep moving. I don't have the patience to stop and turn. The butterflies won't allow it. I'm at their mercy. But my baby girl, my beautiful baby is snug and sleeping. A pang of fear overrides the swarm of butterflies. Please let her be unaffected.

I'd like to stop. I'd like to turn and go home. I would more than anything like to stop, and sit, and be still. If I could, I would trade my youth for the chance to be middle-aged and still. I envy the people passing me in their cars. They are going to work, expected there. I would love to be expected at work, a fifty-year-old. It would be worth the trade to be at peace inside, to do everyday things and be still.

I loved my new house. In the weeks before her birth I would stand in a room and look out of the door to get a view, a new angle to appreciate. Stand. Just stand. Before that I used to go to work. I was expected there. Every day I went to work and came home. I went the next day and I came home. Home: that is what I fear the most.

"What a gorgeous baby. What is her name?"

Help me, help me. (I plead for myself inside.) "Natalie."

"What a lovely name. She's beautiful. You're so lucky."

Help me, help me. "Yes, I am," I smile.

Now I have stopped, I turn and go back home.

I remember it well, that debilitating post-natal anxiety. I used to describe it as having claustrophobia of time. It was horrible – trying to get time to pass, but not being able to make it go quickly enough. I still remember exactly how it felt. And it was that same claustrophobic panic I once experienced with insomnia.

Looking back at myself then makes me realise just how corrosive racing ahead in your thoughts can be, wearing away your ability to be in the present.

Lists and diaries and appointment books are fine unless they start to have a hold over you. Being an ex-insomniac shows me the way to deal with that particular tyranny. The secret, as I see it now, is to put things in the appointments diary and then deal with things as their turn comes up. It's about embracing each thing in the present.

It hasn't been easy getting into it, getting my mind round it, but I'm doing okay. I'm struggling against the tyranny of 'things to do', and having these viewings at Bonchurch makes me even more at the mercy of 'the list'. I find that I really need to slow down and get myself into the moment. I was pleased with myself last night. On my way to Bonchurch Road at 6.30pm I had a wonderful experience: playing music – view over the sea and Brighton from the racecourse – last light of the sunset and lights on across the city – sea a dark, deep blue. Then I really appreciated being there, doing that – there was far more to it than just keeping the appointment. I was in a better frame of mind to meet people and chat, and no longer felt in a hurry – much better.

Non-time

All this came from taking control of time in the night, resting, not worying about being awake. It turned out to be a transferable skill. I practise using my ex-insomniac mindset and I find I can use it more and more in my life.

Nice early start – woke up at 6am after 7 hours sleep. I'm so different now when it comes to making preparations for something the night before, for organising time, but with a different mental background to it. The organising part is practical, rational – what it ought to be, but alongside that I'm enjoying the moment as I do things, rather than racing ahead and seeing the day in units of time/things ticked off or still to be done. It's a real breakthrough. Sometimes things may be forgotten or overlooked, but they will be picked up later when the time comes and it's obvious. I can trust myself that I will think of it, as necessary. If I don't and it becomes a mistake – again I can trust myself to deal with it. Even bad mistakes, and (who knows?) sometimes good can come out of the bad – and I will recognise that, as and when. In other words there's nothing to be frightened of. I can trust myself now and in the future, so the future can be left to take care of itself, in that sense.

As an ex-insomniac I embrace the idea of enjoying the moment. I switch my mindset about not sleeping in the night and I find I'm not lonely when everyone else is asleep. I can reproduce that feeling whenever I want, day or night, in short moments or longer periods of time. When I get in my car, I look forward to having my own company and my music, one of my compilations, favourites from different decades. It settles me, restores my confidence, sets me up for the next thing I'm doing.

I can allow myself to bask in the feeling. I don't have to think ahead. Instead of letting my thoughts race ahead, I can be in the moment, and everything's alright.

It's Pilates later. I've been working on my attitude to getting there and being there – enjoying each part of that; enjoying the body movements, the feel of it all; I used to look at the clock, but don't now. I don't want time to be a factor. If I'm enjoying the moment, time is passing without me noticing at all.

When I'm lost in a book, I am in the moment. I am not racing ahead in my thoughts. I am not thinking of where I am in the book. I am reading for my own pleasure; what page number I'm on, how much I've read or how much left to go are all irrelevant. I read a few pages every day, usually at bedtime, and bit by bit over time it mounts up to an enormous number of books read. I don't notice it. I have read all of those books just in passing.

This is freedom from the time element. It's sustainable – an easy routine I don't have to leave time for or put on my list of things to do. I don't have to think or try. It's natural and relaxed, not forced. It's the same as my attitude to sleep. I don't have to try, I can rest and leave sleep to my body, so I don't have to think about it at all.

There's surprising power in things getting done just in passing. I call it 'non-time'. Here's an everyday example of non-time: I make a cup of tea, then go and have my shower while it's cooling. There's something about showering in tea-cooling time that makes it easier and quicker.

It's hard to be bothered with things I find tedious. And

sometimes that frame of mind becomes quite debilitating. But, hold on, my ex-insomniac skills come to the rescue. Ditch and switch. I can ditch the can't-be-bothered feeling. And switch – cleaning my teeth is time to ponder on a subject of my choice. Now I look forward to spending time with my toothbrush.

An attitude to life that works

I started skiing quite late on in my life – our elder son Richard introduced me to it. It was not long after I left teaching. We've been going for a week to a ski resort (mainly Austria) every year since then, usually around New Year time.

In those first years of skiing I was an insomniac. I remember lying in bed in the chalet-hotel room trying desperately to sleep and desperately to stay calm.

For me at that time sleeplessness had become a condition. "I have this (indeed it has a name) and this is how my life is."

If I think about it now, I could come up with a list of typical unhelpful, counter-productive mindset statements – my practical solutions, as I thought then:

> I do relaxation method in bed and wait for sleep.
>
> I spend all night in sleep mode, being prepared, so sleep can come.
>
> I follow all the dos and don'ts to create a healthy sleep

environment.

I do things that promote a good night's sleep, according to what I have been told/read about

I plan ahead (how to get a message to my ski-school group) for if I don't sleep and can't do the next day.

I was used to insomnia steering events in my life. It had made me leave teaching. And now it was interfering with my skiing. This had to stop.

Q. So what did you do about it?

A. I swapped that hopeless attitude to sleeplessness for one that works. One that breaks the circle. The Insomnia Ditch-and-Switch (yes on reflection I think these words deserve capital letters) It's obvious now. I needed to switch my mindset. And I did. I replaced the mindset that leads to chronic insomnia with the ex-insomniac mindset – an attitude to sleep (and to life) that works.

It works because it's a change of attitude from counter-productive to productive, from negative to positive, from pressurised to liberated.

Everything was different after that. I was in charge – not some vague entity with the name Insomnia that used to be in charge of me.

I made skiing my own after that. One time, after doing well with it during the week in Austria, I decided to go by myself to the Milton Keynes Snozone and practise. It didn't work out too well with the skiing, as I fell and tore my calf muscle. But it was up to me what I took from the experience. I found there were unexpected opportunities:

It was because of the Milton Keynes ski challenge that, as a by-product, I overcame any fears about driving by myself a fairly long distance on the motorway. Now I do it as a matter of course, going to help with the twins – what a wonderful by-product! Things come out of other things unintended.

I realised it's my choice what mindset I have. I can make any situation my own. That's powerful.

8
Alter my angle

My practical voice

I can use my practical voice to cut through the tangle of emotions and get an overview of what I'm stressing about. I know I can do it – I've done it before.

I've been getting a bit emotionally bogged down after RW feedback on my flash-fiction story. Emma had clearly not listened to my story – it wasn't that difficult to follow, was it? Her comments were just ridiculous. But I think there's more to learn from it about myself and keeping a balanced perspective. Dwelling on particular things people said in the meeting and responding emotionally is just self-indulgent (and counter-productive for writing). I need to take the points I find useful and work with those – very good advice. Then I can move forward, not get stuck. I can rise above my negative feelings, get the overview. Ditch the comfort blanket of self-pity.

I can decide I want a different perspective. I am tackling my own mindset directly. Of course, it's not easy. I know it's no quick fix. And it doesn't always seem possible to be practical when I'm having a hard time emotionally. It's hard work getting an overview when I'm right in the thick of it. But it comes with practice, taking each step at a time. I get the feel of building confidence and trusting myself. It's a very good feeling, so I have faith in it. I know I won't go back to how it was before.

It's because I have dealt with insomnia that gives me the confidence to practise being in control. It's the confidence I get from switching my mindset – switching to not having insomnia – and keeping this as my no-doubt knowledge. My bottom line is: I don't have insomnia anymore and it's permanent. This is true for me.

The belief comes from me – I'm doing it on purpose. I control it; it's up to me. It's sustainable because it's irresistible. I love it and I'm sure. I can make things better for myself on purpose. Give things a positive slant by what I say to myself. Be kind to myself, make things easier for myself, but not in a molly-coddling way. It is not an emotional response, like feeling sorry for myself – it is totally different.

When I'm practical, I don't molly-coddle myself. Feeling sorry for myself is too much bother, a waste of my time. Instead of allowing myself to moan or wallow in misery, I can be like another person saying: 'This is going to stop, I'm in charge here. Stop fussing.'

Were someone else to suggest I'm wallowing in self-pity, I'd immediately go on the defensive. Who isn't resistant to personal criticism? But I can tell myself an awful lot that nobody else could get away with. I can speak to my own psyche. Or, the adult can say it to the child in me, if I prefer that way of looking at it. I am then taking charge of my own needs by recognising and responding to the child within. I am being self-reliant, open instead of resistant.

Everyone finds criticism hard to take, especially when it seems so obviously unfair. It feels impossible to rid yourself of the frustration at being unjustly treated or criticised. How can you get it out of your head in the quiet of night? There's no way to change what that person thinks of you, so you're stuck with it, aren't you? No, actually I'm not. I can do an about-face on the situation. I can alter my angle.

A possible strategy is to consider that person's strengths; make myself think in positive terms, however hard it might be! Then consider my own strengths objectively. Everyone has different strengths and it's worth me stopping to think what mine are. Here's an opportunity. Plus, I don't mind being awake, taking these interesting considerations on board. Being objective gives me an overview of the whole situation. Keep that objectivity going. Once I have taken back control, I will not return to the counter-productive ruminating. It feels good turning an obstacle into an opportunity.

My experience of these things tells me it's best to wait until I have turned emotional to practical before I make any responses or decisions. Even responses to unconnected matters are not advisable when I'm under the influence of emotion. As an ex-insomniac I have my own emotional-practical detectors for that. I know when I've ditched my emotion or my self-pity. I know when I'm wearing my matter-of-fact hat again.

As I get to grips with my own psychology, I am gradually developing a sense of mind confidence.

I was thinking about a different word for 'psychology', as it has so many possible interpretations, and it carries with it that mystique which is not helpful. For me, the word 'relationships' seems to cover it just as well: my relationship with others and with myself. Yes, it's more user-friendly and easier to work with. I can be more mind-confident when I make the terms I use my own. It's a way of demystifying. I am renaming those expert terms and tailoring them to my specific needs as only I, myself, can.

Do something active

I've been getting focused on the specific content, rather than getting an overview of my worrying – so I've not been able to rationalise it. I knew the balance was wrong when I confided my worries to M – about pressures people put on me over the weekend – and it sounded really quite extreme. It was obvious then that I had a problem with my stress level over and above the perceived problem – an out-of-control feeling, something obsessional rather than rational.

I may think I'm rationalising it but, if it's an emotional worked-up attempt at rationalising, it's not practical at all. It's actually counter-productive because I'm convincing myself that the content is justified. It goes something like this:

> "This issue is real and important. It warrants my going over it repeatedly and in detail. I need to allow my mind to explore all the implications in case I've missed something. If I try to dismiss it, it just comes back into my head, proving again that's it's a crucial issue."

That's not rationalising, that's molly-coddling my ruminating, wallowing in it. Get a sense of it going too far. Say to myself:

> "The problem now is not the particular issue I've been dwelling on, but my worry, bordering on anxiety. I'll say it bluntly: this is fear. The ruminating gone to excess has shown me this. Next, get my practical voice: already done with 'this is fear'. It's my anxiety, not the issue."

In the night when it's stopping me sleeping I have a sure-fire sign of rumination. During the day it's less clear because I haven't got that indicator. But I can use the same strategies. I can get the emotion out of it and find my practical voice. My inner voice can say:

> "This ruminating is self-indulgent. The problem is my emotive thinking here – letting my thoughts run away with themselves."

It's easier to see this kind of worry thinking in another person. Tackling it in myself can be done though, especially since I'm an ex-insomniac and I've had the practice.

> "Okay, I've recognised my ruminating for what it is – fear. Now I need something that takes me out of myself. What shall I go and do right now?"

I put my coat on, gloves too. I knew it was chilly out there and dark, but I thought I'd put the car away in the underground carpark. If I left it out the windscreen might be iced up in the morning.

I'd turned my ruminating thoughts into one practical idea, something to go and do. Isn't it strange how the content of the worry melts away while you're doing something active like that? Going to the garage must have set in motion those unconscious interweaving threads behind the scenes of my mind. It happened without me thinking anything at all.

Open-minded

Getting an overview is a really important skill for tackling insomnia. It uses the brain's amazing capacity for watching itself. For me it means being able to get a new angle on my emotional response during a sleepless night.

It's a practical way of switching my mindset. I practise altering my angle. So, I'm at the ready. I'm on the alert – prepared at all times (I try!) to look at the other side of the coin.

Insomnia is a fact – if you are an insomniac.

Except that it isn't – when you know otherwise.

When I was an insomniac, I was convinced it was real and unavoidable. I'm an ex-insomniac now. My no-doubt mindset is real and positive, working for me. These are two sides of the same coin. I know which side I prefer.

I see it now. If I'd remained fixed in my mind that having insomnia was a fact, I wouldn't have been able to ditch it. My breakthrough was to stop being an insomniac. Stop that fixed, really unhelpful opinion. Change it. Aha! It was not a fact, not irrevocable. It was alterable.

It's easier to see this sort of thing in other people. You can see when a person's mind is set in a negative, unhelpful way, when they're overly sure of something clearly (in your opinion) erroneous. It's when I see it in myself that I can alter my view and move forward.

The trouble is we so easily form an opinion and then remain fixed on it, as though it is a fact. Our brains tend to work that way. We can sometimes make assumptions based on very little. We often judge situations, other people, ourselves, on scant evidence. We jump to conclusions. We're all like it – it often happens unconsciously. We always want to make links. It's what our brains do – provide us with an easy-to-compute view of a situation.

The good news is that we can alter it. We can alter the conclusion we've jumped to. We can challenge our assumptions. We can bring them to a conscious level and switch to a different viewpoint. We can take charge of our own mode of thinking. For me, that's the ex-insomniac way.

An unexpected turn

Friends used to ask me how my insomnia was and I'd reply, "I don't have insomnia anymore and I never will again." I found this had instant impact – because (at that time) it was unexpected. It's unusual to say 'I don't have insomnia and I never will'. I like the effect it has on myself and on others. I don't say it just for effect though – it's true and that feels great.

I like changing my viewpoint in the middle of a discussion.

"Actually I agree with you now. I've modified my view in the light of your argument." Getting another person's angle on something is quite therapeutic.

More than that. It works on stress like an antidote – if I ditch holding on to being right. Here's an example:

Rog called me a control freak. I couldn't believe the cheek of it. Sitting there partaking of all manner of hospitality from me and then saying that. All because I wanted everyone to stay sitting at the table while I cleared away. I can't tell you how incensed I was. So incensed that I lay awake, incensed, all night!

You can probably guess that was before I became an ex-insomniac. I've thought about it since – along these lines:

> I probably did go too far, insisting nobody could help clear away.
>
> I bet they didn't mind not helping, though.
>
> 'Control freak' trips off the tongue without too much thought.
>
> He may have been saying it in jest.
>
> What was all the fuss about?

Had I thought like that at the time the stress would have fallen away. No sleepless night needed! I was wrong to take it as a personal insult. It's refreshing to be wrong, to admit it to yourself.

I like having the power to change my mind. It's about not being set in my view, keeping an open mind. I can allow myself to be wrong.

Q. Were you wrong when you said you had insomnia?

A. No, I wasn't wrong. I did have it!

Well and truly. I was entrenched in the mindset of being an insomniac. There was no other way of looking at it.

Once I tell myself I have insomnia, my mind becomes programmed to find ways of confirming that viewpoint. It's how our brains work. It's our human nature to want to be proved right: "See how right I was about how bad insomnia is." And that's just what I say to myself. Persuading others needs even stronger proofs. "I told you insomnia was a really bad illness. Do you believe me now, when you can see how dreadfully it has affected my life?"

So it's not easy to tell myself and others the opposite: "I don't have insomnia now." In a way I'm proving myself to have been wrong all along. I have to allow that. It's a case of switching mindset.

Q. If your brain is programmed, how can you get out of it?

A. My brain *becomes* programmed, if I allow it. I can change it, start off the reprogramming. Decide what I want to ditch. Then take a bold mental step. Turn it around. Make the switch. Jump.

If it's insomnia you're ditching, don't have it anymore. Ditch the vicious circle. You don't need it. Switch to being an ex-insomniac. The virtuous circle will come. The confidence and control.

It's refreshing when you take on a different mindset. It has a totally different feel – being in an expansive virtuous circle – after experiencing being in a trap going nowhere except round in circles (maybe even a downward spiral). Being free is a pretty good feeling. And one you want to hold onto.

Part Three
For day-to-day living

Being an ex-insomniac has become an essential part of my life.

And it goes on being useful in all different contexts.

Part Three is about using the Ditch-and-Switch and the ex-insomniac fundamentals in day-to-day living.

9
Connections

Everyone loves an analogy

I use my experience of dealing with insomnia all the time in lots of different ways. I'm used to making connections now as I go along. That's because I've had lots of practice and I like doing it. It works for me.

Here's a question from the author to the reader:

> Q. How is ironing like insomnia?

I'm sensing the answer isn't on the lines of:

> A. There's no connection whatsoever, it's ridiculous.

Would your answer be more along these lines?

> A. It will be an analogy, and I'm waiting to hear all about it with excited anticipation!

Okay, here's the analogy: ironing and insomnia (*note:* author hates ironing)

I could try to make the nightmare of ironing easier by trying to lessen the stress and burden of it. I could think of ways to minimise the pile somehow. Or I could put off doing it as long as possible, although that might make it more stressful, not less. I could get someone to do it for me this time, but that would only be a temporary solution. I could get an ironing company to do it every week, but that would be expensive.

Or what about having no ironing at all? *I don't iron and I never will.* (Are you getting the insomnia parallel yet?) I don't even need to have an iron in the house, if I choose not to. Ditch the ironing pile and everything associated with it. It's much better than always looking for ways to lessen its impact and stress. It's sustainable; I don't have ironing in my life. It's not an issue.

Q. What about creases?

A. I switch my mindset so, along with ironing, creasing is not an issue either.

Ditch thinking of laundry in terms of ironing

Switch to seeing laundry in terms of washing, drying, and folding

Build up tools and strategies e.g. wise choice of fabric when buying clothes; skilful use of tumble dryer and airing cupboard so creases don't form

It doesn't mean I'll never have creasing – but I won't view it as a setback. I'll gain feedback for next time.

My no-doubt mindset is: I don't have ironing in my life anymore, and I never will again.

How similar is that to insomnia!

Snorkelling

Everyone has something they struggle with at some time or another. And, whatever it is, there will be other people all around who find it no trouble at all. Take flying in a plane. Some people are afraid of it and others do it without a second thought.

It happens to everyone; you find yourself in a situation where you are the one who's afraid and others aren't. You feel disempowered and frustrated by what is lacking in yourself. It's the nature of being a human being to compare ourselves to others. It's what we do.

We are all different and unique. We have things we can do and like to do: games, sport, all kinds of interests and activities. It's our own thing. On the other hand there are those things we cannot do, but would really like to be able to do.

For me, snorkelling was one of those things. For ages I'd felt that I should be able to do it, and could, if only I weren't so scared. I'd been frustrated about it for years.

But it's a different story now. I am an ex-insomniac. I had the feeling snorkelling was like sleeping – I could tackle it like I tackled insomnia.

So here we go. An ex-insomniac's take on snorkelling – written on the beach in Tobago:

> *Back to the beginning, first snorkel of the holiday*
>
> *Ditch things first: fussing/routine – what I look like, hair – get it wet (regardless of meeting the rep at 11am). Important – get out of routine (ditch the tyranny of it). Small things add up to a big difference*

Does that remind you of anything – the sleeping environment maybe and ditching all those fussy details?

> *My first thoughts on snorkelling again:*
>
> *Straight in this time No fear then? No, it's gone – that's in the past.*

What factors made this come about? It's about making it my own:

> *I'm not dependent on M for safety, for confidence, as before. I'm sure – sure of the situation/sure of myself in that situation. Memories of panic (find a better word; there are levels of 'panic', a scale) Do I have an overview of where I'm going (here it's literal)? Or am I dependent on M to have that? No, not now – I'm in charge, in control.*
>
> *I know what I used to be like: Where am I going to get out of the water? What exactly will I do? What if there's a problem? That's the big unhelpful mode of thinking: what if.... Therein lies an endless chain of fear – when I race ahead in my thoughts.*

> *But I can stop it now – on the first level of the scale – easy. I recognise each particular 'what if' and don't bother with it. Instead I go back to the moment.*
>
> *I know I'm covered. I can bask in this feeling of being alright.*

It's a perfect analogy with the ex-insomniac take on the sleep situation, don't you think? The fears I used to have but have eliminated now. The feeling of being in control, making it my own. And there's more to come.

Snorkelling with flippers:

> *More learning opportunities – significant extra details re making it my own Practising/getting more ordinary details/experiences under my belt e.g. can tread water in a relaxed way and take my mouth piece out to talk. Similar examples with sleeping are: no special pillow/don't have to read to fall asleep (and loads more)*

Snorkelling without fins: (note subtle change of vocabulary, as author becomes snorkelling expert!)

> *Feeling the ebb and flow of the waves, the swell towards the rocks with a little force. Entry-level panic? No. There are choices. Can go with the flow and allow myself to b e carried along effortlessly. Or swim against the flow and put in the effort. Both work. I decide, my choice, I'm in charge. It's a good feeling.*

I have the same kind of control in the sleep situation. I have choices – it's up to me.

We went in a glass-bottomed boat to see the coral. The snorkelling, though, was disappointing – not so much to see as here in the hotel reef. But I carried on adding skills, knocking down more barriers: significant step for me, getting into deep water to snorkel off the boat, putting flippers on while treading water, snorkelling away from boat and out of sight of M briefly (but kept risks in mind e.g. don't swim too far away on your own), taking photo of M underwater (shame I had my finger over lens!). No nerves with all this, just practicalities. Comes from taking each step at a time (all the time during the day), instead of thinking ahead and trying to pre-prepare (not practical at all). Yes, that's straight from my ex-insomniac mindset. Swam under rope from boat to anchor – had brief panicky feeling about this (nervy memory of a past experience) – preferred M to hold up rope for me. But didn't allow the panicky feeling to get a grip – controlled it

Q. How do you control a panicky feeling?

A. Recognise it and nip it in the bud – turn panicky to practical.

Stopped at Englishman's Bay on the way back, where we snorkelled for a short time until M thought there might be risks (changing currents, bags unattended on beach). But I was very pleased with myself for going in where there were waves crashing and quite a swell. As I dipped below the surface, I could hear my breathing, rhythmic and comforting. I was on my own with it, aware of my body's movement, in the moment.

I'm not afraid now. Overcoming lots of small fears by observing/ modifying details has allowed me to overcome the general fear. I'm not nervous, I'm practical. What a difference that makes. Definite insomnia parallel there

You can tell I was proud of myself. Through practice I had internalised the strategies for tackling insomnia and now I was using the same skills for tackling snorkelling.

Q. Can you recap on what they are?

A. Yes, they are the Ditch-and-Switch strategies:

> Ditch fussy routines and nip each small fear in the bud.
>
> Switch from nervous to practical and keep the overview.
>
> Ditch what-ifs (racing ahead in my thoughts, trying to pre-prepare).
>
> Switch to being in the moment. Let my body go with the flow.

Bit by bit I internalise the learning. I take on board the skills and strategies. I practise and make it my own. So I am doing the fundamental things really well.

Q. Like the fundamentals for sleep: I allow my body to decide about sleep; it doesn't matter if I'm awake; I don't have insomnia anymore and it's permanent?

A. Yes, that's right.

Open-ended

Well then, what can I take from my notes on snorkelling and

the insomnia parallels?

Can the same strategies be used in all different activities? It's not a system, though, not tick boxes. That's important to remember. It's an open-ended learning process. I wonder if I can replicate that process with skiing. My fear has always spoilt my time on the slopes, getting in the way of my progress and enjoyment. It has been a source of great frustration to me.

I realise for a start that there is no point trying to figure out why I was scared of snorkelling. I'm glad I didn't waste any time on that. And it's the same with skiing. Deal with the nerves directly and the underlying causes of the fear will dissipate of their own accord – just as it happened with insomnia.

I realise too that I now take snorkelling for granted – my body deals with it at the time. I don't have to think about it in advance. Only to make sure I have a mask, snorkel and appropriate stretch of water!

Another significant realisation: after ditching insomnia I was moving towards natural sleep but it was not my goal. And yes it was the same with snorkelling – I was moving towards natural snorkelling and I didn't have a goal with that either.

I've been sitting out on the balcony in the October sun – so lucky, but it's very windy and I've had to admit too chilly. Besides, my pages were waving about too much to write on them. I was out there trying to note down some thoughts on Zen in the Art of Archery (as you do!). I read the book a while ago – I recommended it in relation to snooker. It was written 90 years ago by a German professor who trained with a Zen master in Japan. My notes/ thoughts: I sensed a connection between the archer practising his art, discovering something about himself – this is his aim, not the target – and my enjoyment of no longer having a fixed goal but being on an expansive open-ended path. Something about being outside with the elements, I think, added to my pleasure at glimpsing the Zen philosophy and finding a reflection of my own ex-insomniac way.

With insomnia I liked not having a goal – a cure to make me sleep. Natural sleep – my body taking care of it – was far more relaxing! With snorkelling too I liked being laid-back about it, no target to achieve.

This was my ex-insomniac mindset evolving; I was on a continuum. Expansive. Not fixed and contained like a goal.

Q. But goals are useful, aren't they?

A. Yes, often they are.

Of course we have goals and targets, and of course we want results, perhaps a cure. Everyone seeks solutions to life's problems, and mostly we need our answers to be direct and easy to achieve. We want to tick boxes. We want to place people and situations in easily recognised slots. Everyone does it. It's part of day-to-day living – the brain's need to categorise and make sense of things.

But sometimes having a goal and ticking it off when you're done is the opposite of what the brain is comfortable with. It doesn't work with insomnia – needing a result is guaranteed to stop you sleeping. I know this to be true from my insomniac nights.

And I know – since I've been an ex-insomniac – that life throws up situations where sustainability is needed – where you need tried and tested tools. My ex-insomniac mindset gives me ongoing managing strategies and I use them over and over again in the day as well as night in all different contexts.

I think a table would come in useful at this point:

Fixed	Open-ended
Goal	Continuum
Target	Fundamentals
Cure	Natural sleep
Aim	Expansive
Result	Sustainable
Box ticked	Evolving

Once I got the feel of being on a continuum, I started finding connections all over the place:

Then I did the voice-coaching lesson with the CD – finding my middle voice. Think I'm on the continuum now. Related to sleeping, it's to do with natural sleep – allowing. My body will find its own path: like my voice will naturally want to find the middle.

On my way up the drag lift I relaxed into the moment – part of that was curling up my toes and feeling the different parts of each foot, as we do in Pilates. It helped me to tune in to my body. As I skied down, I felt the natural inclination for my legs to be parallel, and for the weight to change from one foot to the other. That coincided with a different sound of my skis on the snow, the edges cutting in. I had a sense of being on the same continuum as advanced skiers. That's because I allowed my body to feel its way – I went with it a bit more each time.

10
Challenge

Taking on fear

I am not afraid of snorkelling anymore. How did I do it? I nipped panic in the bud.

What is this panic thing? I certainly didn't see it as panic at the time. I would have been really defensive if someone had suggested it. "Of course I'm not panicking. Don't be ridiculous." But I was.

I wanted to look into this word/concept 'panic'. It was interesting now, fascinating in fact. We use the word 'panic' all the time. I often want to say, 'Don't panic' to myself or another person. But I didn't want to use it now. It wasn't clear enough what I meant. It's funny how a word becomes meaningless when it covers too large a range of meaning.

For a start, I needed a word to describe a mild panicky feeling. And I wanted to trace where mild panicky feelings led if they were not nipped in the bud. That seemed important. I was on a mission. I needed some sort of scale.

Here's the one I came up with:

Low level	Medium	Full-on
Unsettled/unsure	Nervy	Fear
Nervous	Very nervous	Dread
Mild butterflies	Strong butterflies	Inner turmoil
Voicing uncertainty	Voicing fear	Voiceless
On the verge of tears	Crying/moaning	Screaming
Sweaty	Profuse sweating	Sweat turns to cold
Want to get away	Urge to get away	Lose track of place
Tense up	Verge of losing control	Lose control/faint
Dry mouth	Nausea	Sickness
Apprehensive	Fear of a threat	Terror

I wanted to consider the high-level panic too. With insomnia I had the scary experience of hallucinating and also being on the brink of a panic attack. What do I make of all that now, looking back from my perspective as an ex-insomniac?

I looked up panic attack symptoms on the internet. I wanted to consider all the possibilities in the range of panic. I read about the symptoms and the explanations behind them.

It said of palpitations: adrenalin release into the blood stream makes your heart race; it will not harm you. Do not give it credibility and it will go. Chest pain is caused by muscle tension, not a heart attack. We shake when nervous or cold, due to spasmodic muscle contractions; that's normal and it will pass. Weakness in the arms and tingling in the hands and feet are the body's reaction to the fright-and-flight impulse, affecting circulation, blood oxygen and carbon dioxide levels – not harmful; it will return to normal. Hallucinations are a transient symptom, but can be frightening if not understood.

I noticed as I read that I wasn't afraid of these symptoms anymore. They had been beautifully decoded and demystified.

Everyone is irrationally afraid of something – things which others do not fear at all. And we see others panicking about something we take in our stride. My friend has a fear of flying, whereas I think nothing of it. Isn't it funny how different we are? And yet we're all in the same boat really (transport connection unintended).

People certainly have fear with insomnia: anxiety as bedtime approaches; finding it scary in the night; worry about the next day; superstitious thoughts about what will stop you sleeping; stress bordering on panic. I was a chronic insomniac. I recognise all that.

My mission statement:

> I am an ex-insomniac. I take on fear. I recognise and understand the levels of panic on the scale. I nip panic in the bud. Being practical I take the mystery and inevitability out of fear and panic.

A small but significant realisation —

I now mistrust my own nerviness – it is very unreliable as a signal; nerviness is not always connected with a worrying situation. But that is exactly what happens. One's nervous system doesn't recognise the difference between real and imaginary situations – or if it's not a situation at all, real or imaginary, but simply a physiological occurrence. I realise now that I should override my nerviness, stay mentally aloof from it, and think practically. I find the nerviness goes away when I don't heed it. But it needs practice to do that, because we are well programmed to expect our nervous system to mirror our fears, real ones. I feel this is quite a breakthrough for me. Now I can deal with the nervy tummy separately, like an ache or pain, or indigestion or something, and not let it make me actually nervous or worried.

I had figured out something about how nerviness operates, and that understanding gave me control of my nervy reactions. It was liberating and really helped me move forward.

Back home – long, long sleep last night, following sleep during the evening as well. So I'm well rested now. I still don't count the night without sleep as insomnia, because of my attitude to it. It did not worry me at the time, as I knew I would be okay whatever, and I think I understand why it happened: my nervous system has not caught up with my new attitude. It still reads the circumstances as worrying: alarm set for 6.30am, packing to finish off, travel arrangements, will I cope without sleep?, stayed up late ignoring having to get to bed, not giving myself time to prepare and plan ahead. All these elements are what my nervous system is familiar with, and used to respond with worry and insomnia. These were all the elements that led to my original insomnia, and my nervous system has responded the same way ever since. It has not caught up yet with this reaction being no longer required. When it gets used to my body not acknowledging/needing its response/ warning, it will gradually ease off with its reaction.

Take on challenge, take on nerves

Taking on challenge and taking on nerves go hand in hand. It's about facing the challenge of going out of my comfort zone and gently but decisively tackling how my nervous system reacts.

I'm proceeding with the nervy ski syndrome – working on the effects of challenge on the nervous system. I started to work on the snorkelling last week, testing out my new snorkel in the pool. I'm working on ski technique by reading the Learning to Ski book and keeping my ski boots out. I want to think up some other challenges to keep up the momentum of pushing myself, doing things out of my comfort zone. I want to have a nervy tummy and see it as adrenalin, rather than steer clear of it – rather than trying to make the nervousness go away by ditching the challenge and avoiding the activity. It's all very interesting. I'm regarding myself like a case study.

Once I'd put my panic scale together it suggested strategies for dealing with the feelings. I came up with observing my nerviness. I rated how nervous I was on a scale of 0–10. This works in practice surprisingly well, and I found that monitoring myself in this way was very interesting. Otherwise nerves are very boring.

In Austria, Thursday –

I'm sitting in the family room on a comfy sofa, looking out of the balcony doors onto a very close snow-covered mountainside, blue sky above with cumulus cloud and sun on the slope. I have my bottle of water on the coffee table and yesterday's newspaper which I've just bought in the supermarket (glad to find English papers on sale). I also bought a tin of vegetable soup for my lunch (I can heat it up in the family-room microwave – excellent forward planning on my part!) and two brown rolls.

I was just sitting at the table eating my second bowl of soup with my second brown roll, when I suddenly thought, "What time is it?", and looked quickly at my watch. This action was accompanied by a burst (fairly mild but distinguishable) of nerviness. "Where's this horrible (but familiar) feeling coming from?" I wondered.

My next thought was, "All I'm doing is meeting J downstairs in the boot room." Followed by, "I've internalised the ex-insomniac message and I'm only doing what I want to do, in the way I want to do it. I'm in charge of myself." That was an antidote to the nerviness. Instant

Feedback from it –

As my renewed introduction to skiing got closer and closer, I started to find ways of getting out of it. Or my psyche did. How weird! My psyche wants to create resistance.

What a bloody cheek! I'm not having that, not if I, Nicki Gillard, can help it. I'll put paid to any nerviness by focusing on the task in hand. Starting with putting my ski boots on, which I'm off to do now…

In Austria, Friday: feedback on my skiing

I can say more or less I'm taking it in my stride. All but a couple of times I was doing only practical planning in my head. I got rid of the what-ifs pretty much as they jumped into my mind – I was ready for them and nipped them in the bud.

Focusing on my nerviness turns into relaxation. Isn't that an interesting paradox? Being with my nerves – having them where I can see them – means I can truly relax, because they're not going to take me by surprise, which is how they (insidiously) operate.

My nervy tummy has a superb memory. It's uncanny how it knows when to intervene, when to manifest itself. Nerves are very cunning. They have a repertoire, a modus operandi of great variety. For example, they tell me that I can't eat; that I feel ill or tired; that I need to keep looking at the time, etcetera. They create resistance and avoidance in countless clever ways, but especially if they can catch me unawares and make me panicky.

That relies on the element of surprise. Keep guard by focusing on my nerviness: where is it? What exactly is it doing? What method is being used now at this present moment?

Unless of course I'm too busy doing and I'm not thinking. That's the worst thing for my nerves – they can't abide that. It renders them obsolete.

R and Julia were talking about skiing and fear. I said my fear had gone and they thought that was not helpful to artificially create a situation where I felt no fear. They said some fear is natural and necessary. Accept it – it keeps you safe. Then I remembered there was a point where I was going faster than I wanted across the slope and it took time for my technique to slow me down. Crucially I didn't panic – there's a fine line I recognise – it's about keeping my nerve. My fear hadn't gone. It was with me, but this time channelled into my body moving across the slope.

I've used that mantra before. Keep my nerve. As an ex-insomniac I understand how to recognise that fine line, how to master it and not let being unnerved tip into panic. Stay focused on what my body is doing.

J was saying about how top sports people take the pressure, mix it in with their nerves inside the body, and release it as positive energy and inspiration.

I think I'm doing quite well in my own sporty way!

Ditch-and-Switch in the daytime

Stress is a challenge. It can strike at any time (as insomnia might strike an insomniac), sparked off by anything: an email, something quite minor going wrong, a criticism out of the blue, being left out. Any insignificant event can do it.

I was waiting to be served in a cafe in the Needlemakers in Lewes – sitting at a small table in the far corner. I'd previously gone up to the counter but was told by a waitress to sit down and someone would come to take my order. Except they didn't. The server guy went over to a couple who'd come in after me. The stress of being ignored rose to the surface. I called out, 'Excuse me', but was not heard. I went over to the counter and oh so nicely requested my order be taken. When I got back to my seat I could have cried to let out the pounding stress within.

I didn't cry and I didn't carry on suffering the stress. I have the ex-insomniac determination to stop it, to nip it in the bud. I ditched the vicious circle of stress and insomnia, didn't I? I used the same skills here. I have been practising the Ditch-and-Switch at bedtime and it works just as well during the day.

I got the overview and recognised my body's stress reaction. I replaced emotional with practical. And I was alright. My mind-switch created a virtuous circle. I knew when I was in it, when I'd jumped the vicious one. I was pleased with myself for doing that, for rising to the challenge.

Getting the overview is like looking down on myself. A bird's-eye view. (Not an out-of-body experience. Much more down-to-earth than that). The brain can do this. It can flip to watching itself, to being aware of what it is doing. It can do a switch or a ditch or a Ditch-and-Switch any day or night.

It comes in very handy when you're beside yourself with

stress and you need something powerful to find your way out of it. This happened to me when I wanted to change my phone recently —

The stress has hit me completely unawares. I can't believe how horrible it feels, way beyond what makes sense; it's like I've been taken over by it. But I'm an ex-insomniac – I'll do something. Walk. Walk around the block. Forget the delivery and the mistake and the whole saga of bad luck and incompetence preceding it. Yes, as soon as possible look beyond all that stuff. It's the stress I have to deal with right now. Keep walking, not ready to go in yet, a different way round this time, so it's still interesting. The stress is there inside me. I can feel it like a ball in my gut. Not very nice, but better than in my head. It's like indigestion or heart burn or something. Four times round the block and I'm back in. The stress has gone.

Choices

Being an ex-insomniac equips me to steer myself through difficult times (some harder than problems with phones!). I'm gradually getting to know what to say and not to say to myself. I choose what I want to ponder over. I do all that on purpose, because I did it with insomnia when I made positive, optimistic choices.

I realised there are different kinds of choices I can make for myself. Allowing my body to decide is a laid-back kind of choice. Nipping negative thoughts in the bud is a very active choice – a definite action. It feels good to be in charge of my mood like that, to know exactly what I'm doing – affecting my own physiological reactions.

I can de-stress by doing things on purpose to lighten my mood. Sometimes it needs a quick turn-around: "Okay, I'll do a John-on-the-beach."

Or I might feel a more gradual, relaxed process would suit my mood better: "So I'll be patient, slow things down and be in the moment."

Good evening at RW, J there too. I came home feeling a bit heavy in a ruminating sort of way, which is hard to describe but familiar. There's something about the RW meetings that provokes this feeling in me. (J may get a bit like it too.) It's probably because you put yourself on the line, not only when you read out your work, but also when you say things about others' work. You lay yourself open in a way which is particular to that situation. Is this a case for needing a thicker skin? It didn't affect me sleeping – I am over that now. I just observed myself and my feelings and allowed them to be aired/go away in a good balance, not being impatient but recognising the gradual process. A balance of accepting and working on being proactive. Also trusting that the feelings will balance out, and not heeding the physiological reactions – that 'heavy in a ruminating sort of way', which is akin to nerviness, and which I have learnt to mistrust.

Sometimes it's about choosing a more relaxed viewpoint. That might mean challenging my own mindset in order to see an issue in a different way. It might mean being hard on myself, in order to be kind to myself in the end. For example: I'm going over and over a troublesome issue involving blaming another person. How can I get myself off the hook here? Only when I've truly considered my own part in the matter: "I can see where I have a share in the blame for what happened. I know now what I'm letting myself off the hook for." The stress falls away like magic after that.

Or I might choose to use stress in the night for research purposes. With the kind of stress where my brain just won't keep still and there doesn't seem to be any one issue that needs my attention, I may as well use it to get feedback on how I'm dealing with it. That's taming the stress, taking control of it.

If I rename stress as adrenalin, it creates a totally different feel. Sometimes adrenalin can be excitement, or a lesser version of that – along a spectrum. That really helps me when I'm awake with an over-active mind. By renaming it, I'm making it my own, de-mystifying it.

I've been making my mindset my own – at first out of necessity in tackling insomnia and then out of wider interest, engaging more with myself, with others and with the world in general. Making something my own, I've come to realise, is a way of taking the pressure off in all kinds of situations – it really works. I'm figuring things out and simplifying, giving myself knowledge I may have assumed only an expert could have. I'm making myself the expert.

In a way I am researching who I am, because dealing with insomnia puts me in the position of focusing positively on myself and making choices for myself. I am exploring how I want to be. Being an ex-insomniac gives me that focus and points me in that optimistic direction. I can give myself more and more focus, if I want to let it evolve.

Q. Is that egocentric?

A. No, I don't believe it is.

In the days when I was an insomniac I was more likely to view the sleep situation in an egocentric way. When I was suffering, I became fixed on my own inward-looking viewpoint. Mine was the correct view; other positions were different from mine, therefore incorrect. But as an ex-insomniac I look outwards beyond my own emotional view.

Now I'm more likely to see similarities rather than differences between my own viewpoint and others'. I like finding a point of contact, a connection.

Pressure's off

I affirmed I wasn't trying to get to sleep, but allowing my body to decide, and in the meantime I actively (ruminating is more passive – it happens to you) let my mind explore the issue unemotionally and range over other subjects too. I woke up in the middle of the night with a repeat – the issue popped into my head and I was immediately awake with it. I got up and had a drink of water (4am), and did the same thing; this time bringing in the thought about having first sleep and later on second sleep. I woke up at 7am.

I read an article in the paper about people in the past regularly having two phases of sleep. This really takes the pressure off. It seems to be very common; I wake up and have a fairly prolonged time awake before my next sleep. It's relaxing to know that's perfectly acceptable. My body can decide about all that, so I don't have to concern myself.

I choose to take charge of my own thoughts and emotions. I want to take the pressure off myself. I am making life easier for myself on purpose.

'Get your head out of it' is so important for tackling ruminating in the night. I know that from last night. But it seems impossible to control what my mind is doing. I know I would be sleeping otherwise, because I'm really tired. The only way is to get my head into it, but in a different, non-ruminating way. Assert, 'I'm not trying to get to sleep' and it doesn't matter if I'm awake. Once those mantras have taken the place of the persistent, troublesome issue, everything is different. I've made the switch and it fundamentally alters my mindset. I only realise it's worked when I wake up! But that informs the next time. Take off the pressure, in other words. It's actually easier than tackling the issue directly, if I've gone too far into being stressed by it – which was the case with me last night. This morning it's still frustrating, and would continue to be, if I weren't off shortly to start another busy day.

Situations don't change by using ex-insomniac strategies, but it helps a great deal when the stress of them isn't mixed in with sleep issues. Knowing I don't have insomnia, and never will, is a wonderful antidote to stress.

Now I'll just ignore it and move on. I'm glad I have my ex-insomniac mindset on being awake – that means I can move on because I wasn't adversely affected by the sleeplessness side of the ruminating. The mindset is second nature to me now – not sleeping really isn't an issue – so that cancels out a large element of what might have been a vicious circle – the ruminating on its own is far less corrosive.

No vicious circle – how wonderful! Thank goodness I've

realised: insomnia isn't the serious insoluble problem I used to think it was. I'm not stuck with it forever, waiting for a cure. I even make light of it now. Put it well and truly in its place.

It's made me realise too that I can make refreshing changes. And I find I can do that again and again. In any situation. It's become a natural thing to take the pressure off myself and to lift my spirits as I go along.

I keep using the open-ended sustainable strategies – the ex-insomniac basics – all the time.

Ok I've got my plan and timing in place to include the viewing in one property and the washing machine delivery on the other side of town. What can go wrong? I'll play it by ear. (Good idea to measure downstairs entrance for access) If it does go wrong, I'll just deal with it unemotionally. This kind of thing is like practice. If any future creative plans are going to be doable and sustainable, obstacles (there will inevitably be many and of varied kind) have to be met and overcome with as little stress as possible. At first yesterday M's reaction to the plumbing obstacle made me feel stressed towards him, as I was dealing with it practically. But later (as I drove home) I used strategies to be calm about M's stress. Plus, he left a very helpful message – he'd calmed himself down too.

It often happens that you think you've coped with other people's stress during the day – you've had to be the opposite, absolutely calm and unemotional.

Q. So did I manage to stay stress-free? Or was I outwardly calm, just pushing my stress inside?

A. It's impossible to know.

Q. How does that help me if it's the bottled-up type of stress and it comes out when I get to bed or wake up in the night?

A. I don't need to know actually. My thinking is:

I don't do causes or triggers – the nature of the stress is irrelevant to me, and unfathomable anyway, so forget it.

I fall back on my ex-insomniac mantras and sleep is not an issue. I take sleep for granted. I allow the natural and stick to the basics – it doesn't matter if I'm awake; I don't have insomnia anymore; my body decides about sleep. The vicious circle is deprived of its oxygen – it doesn't have stress about being awake to keep it going – and it fizzles out. Good riddance!

So I keep going with the virtuous circle. I know how it works. I allow my mind and body to work together. I have control of my mindset and I leave sleep to my body. This is a continuous, sustainable path. Sustainable means reliable. I sense my progress along a continuum – in any context I like. I know I can keep going with the ex-insomniac mindset and trust it.

11
Creative Energy

Attack back

I was just getting my car out of the underground carpark yesterday when I got a real feeling of nerviness, like an attack. A few things came at me all at once – a couple of problems, a sudden pang of worry. It's amazing how bad these stress sensations can be. I leapt up the panic scale in an instant – pounding heart, a flush of dread, sudden sickening nerviness.

"Where did that come from? What's the matter with me?" In the rush of my thoughts I make false links; I misinterpret, blame; I jump to conclusions. A vicious circle gets going so quickly and easily. One thought leads to another. It determines the way I think and feel, dictating, like a tyrant, what course it takes. Unless – aha! – I recognise the call for a Ditch-and-Switch:

"Hold on, I've been here before, and I don't like it – letting my gut feeling dictate how I will feel next. I can alter that course, and I know it will make all the difference. No, my gut feeling will not be in charge."

Of course I associate my dread with the problem on my mind. I trust that association, take it as read. It's true and real, not a figment of my imagination of course; the bodily sensations are very real indeed.

But the association is false – this is what I've got to stop. I can stop it. See its falseness and ditch it. Don't put up with it; be proactive, have a strategy. I am an ex-insomniac, motivated to do what works.

I switch my attitude to it. I will not be scared. I know what to do.

And what not to do. I don't do waste-of-time causes/triggers for a start. This is not about dealing directly with what's stressing me – the actual content of it. I can't do that now – not when the stress has piled up on me like this and hit me unawares.

I tell myself: okay these sensations are very strong. But that doesn't mean my worries are great. They are certainly not symptoms of some unidentified medical problem. (How non-productive that line of worrying would be!)

No, the dread is an unwanted and unneeded physiological reaction – no more than that. And it can be ditched. Instead I will deal with the bodily sensations that come with it.

Q. How?

A. Provide an instant antidote. Do something physical – on the spot or go somewhere. Just move about anyhow. Attack the anxiety.

I drove to Ovingdean to send the parcels, then back down to park the car and, instead of going indoors, went to get my therapy: exercising my body, the one and only antidote I know for nerviness. I attacked back. Spurning the mown pathways, I strode cross-country up the hill towards the bench at the top. I was in the Falklands, yomping over the tussock grass, the fresh, chilly wind on my face and the views of farmland in front of me, or across the sea if I stopped and looked around. Of course it worked – it always does. My nerviness disappeared. I just had to remember that – and I did this time.

When I return to the problems later, the gut association will not be there, and I can deal with them practically. Problems that had piled up on me previously, creating one unwieldy load, will be separate ones now. Some may not even be problems at all. And some I will tackle with the addition of creative thinking.

If I want I can come back to a particular worry later. Anything like that (something that grabs me unawares and throws me into worry/anger/frustration mode) is best tackled when I'm in a practical frame of mind anyway. It needs to be out of my mind for a bit in order for that to happen.

Q. Aren't you just brushing the problem under the carpet and denying your true emotion?

A. I can't rely on my gut reaction to tell me the truth. I decide how I want to play it, as I did with insomnia.

The main thing is not to be at the mercy of my emotions. I can't stop my feelings, if something has made me sad or angry or frustrated. But I can alter the way I respond to them. I can stop the stressing by ditching and switching.

It's great that my ex-insomniac strategies are always there to fall back on, giving me confidence and control.

And it's very satisfying to have turned wasteful stress into productive energy.

Taming adrenalin

When I was an insomniac, adrenalin was enemy number one. It was the unstoppable fuel of that relentless activity invading my brain in the night.

It's not my enemy now, because I've worked out how it operates. I know adrenalin can either work for me or against me. I never knew I could actually be in charge of it. I had no idea about turning things around. I had not ditched insomnia then.

Now I know quite a bit about adrenalin. I've tamed it – made it my own. Here's what I have learnt from my personal experience of it:

→ Sometimes I can ditch the stress-type adrenalin and switch it to excitement. It's not as difficult as it sounds, because these two apparent opposites are actually very closely linked. Lots of times it's just a question of realising I can make the switch. Say to myself, "Oh, that's not stress-adrenalin. It's excitement." It feels much better calling it that and, as we know, words and concepts can be changed in one fell swoop.

I need to work on how I interpret my nerves – embrace them in a way. Don't think in terms of a threatening experience, more a pleasurable one. It reminds me of how J and I dealt with the big wheel at the fair – we turned fear (wanting to escape) into excitement (encouraging the feeling, wanting it). It's turning it around (no pun intended, honestly) like doing a John-on-the-beach.

→ Once I have switched to that mindset, I can turn excitement into calm enjoyment, if I prefer it that way, and then I can be in the moment.

Things are exciting when there's no agenda in the mind, nothing required to happen. Excitement is spontaneous; it's about being in the moment, enjoying myself. It can turn into calm satisfaction – not spilling over into euphoria; as an ex-insomniac I know how counter-productive that can be. Over-excitement goes with quick fixes and is so often followed by disappointment. That feeling of anti-climax is quite depressing. You don't get it when there is sustainability. Being an ex-insomniac has that permanence; you lift your mood in tandem with your mindset. It's a pretty good package.

If I prefer to let my natural euphoria flow freely that's okay too. It's up to me.

→ Adrenalin fuels ruminating – that's the over-active brain syndrome everyone has from time to time. The thing is to recognise it, get an overview of it. Then I can stop it in its tracks.

I'm trying to get to grips with the ruminating. It's not stopping me sleeping, but I woke up with the nagging, quite unpleasant feelings this morning. The memory of how it feels comes first, then the actual issues kick in and I'm wide awake with it. I have to get up at that point, because the nice waking-up-slowly moment has gone. I don't want to grapple with the actual content – that's more ruminating. I want to get an overview of it. Then I can turn the negative to positive, be in control rather than at the mercy of these feelings. First, deal with what adjustments I can effect, practical ones, and then come up with ideas/plan of attack

Ditch the ruminating and switch to overview. Use the adrenalin for creative ideas.

→ But this is not always possible, especially in the middle of the night when the flow of adrenalin is particularly strong (for whatever reason – and it's no use bothering to even think what's produced it). The adrenalin stops me getting anywhere near finding creative energy. At a time like that I can simply reassure myself: being awake is not insomnia, everything's alright – leave sleep to my body.

I can see why I was awake most (seemed like all) of Saturday night. The build-up of small tensions over the week, combined with the perceived pressure on me at the weekend, was causing the hard-to-shift adrenalin invasion, which is so familiar; and goes back to dire insomnia days. I did well not to let it turn into worse stress. I stayed practical, trying to rationalise the more obvious issues that my mind was dwelling on and think of one practical step. But it was not possible to relax enough. What I could do, though, was to affirm I'm not trying to sleep/doesn't matter if I'm awake/I don't have to worry because my body will decide about sleep. That's the doable/sustainable part to fall back on. Kept me emotion-free, in spite of the stresses

→ Sometimes adrenalin isn't really that negative; I'm just stimulated, not stressed. It often happens after a night out. My brain is still active when I get to bed. It's not unpleasant in itself, but it becomes unpleasant because I now want to sleep. I'm surprised I'm not sleeping because it's late, very late – I am tired and it's definitely sleep time. But my brain refuses to cooperate. 'Have I got a problem with adrenalin? You're supposed to sleep better after alcohol. Everyone says so. It must be me – a sleep problem.' Now it's turned to stress.

Q. 'Help, how do I switch my brain off?'

A. Recognise what type of adrenalin it is, relax and go along with it. Don't try to sleep. Fall back on the ex-insomniac mantras: 'I don't have insomnia. It doesn't matter if I'm awake. I'll leave it to my body to decide about sleep.'

It's like having a safety net. However stressed I may be I always have my ex-insomniac mindset. Armed with that, I can choose how to play it. It all depends on the situation and how I'm feeling. I can bring about the changes I want because I'm in charge of myself.

Adrenalin stimulates creativity, so don't be afraid of it. Tame it, make it my/your own. I stopped being afraid of not sleeping. I took away its scariness by my attitude to it, by renaming it, by seeing it differently. I know I can do the same with adrenalin.

Tools for the job

Ex-insomniacs gather tools. Not quick fixes. Tools are for permanence. And I still get instant results when I want. I use the John-on-the-beach tool any time in any situation, whenever I want to ditch and switch. It's always at my disposal – it has sustainability. The great thing is that my insomnia learning experience can be related to any other area of life. I can use the same strategies and gradually develop a repertoire of tools, ready to recruit when the need arises.

I borrowed the word 'recruit' from my Pilates teacher. She uses it when talking about muscles. I thought this was an interesting connection – muscles are a kind of tool. Particular muscles are recruited by the body according to their function, just as I, as an ex-insomniac, select my tools for the job.

I feel a list coming on:

> Tools
>
> the Insomnia Ditch-and-Switch
>
> giving myself feedback
>
> finding balance

renaming

using mantras

cherry picking

seeing analogies

changing viewpoint

I'm gradually getting a sense of the tools I have in my repertoire and how they can be used in my life.

The mantra 'not racing ahead' evolved as I got on with day-to-day living. I'd been carrying over strategies from the sleep situation into my life generally. Reminding myself to slow down inside, instead of racing ahead, made a huge difference.

Not racing ahead. I use this so much now. It's become one of my mantras. 'Don't race ahead in my thoughts' encapsulates a lot of the important thought processes about time, being in the moment, trusting myself. I have nothing to be afraid of. I will deal with whatever happens as and when the need arises. I know in myself that I will find a way forward. Knowing that, I can leave the future to take care of itself and deal with the present. No need to prepare for eventualities – only where it's more practical to do so.

I create my own tools and use them in my own way. I tailor them to suit my purposes. Using tools is really the same as having strategies or developing skills. It's all part of the same thing. For me, it's the ex-insomniac way of being mind-flexible, finding my creative energy – and enjoying life.

Playing

Talking of enjoying life, we can learn a lot about that from seeing how children play.

Children make the world their own through play. When young children draw a picture, listen to a story, play with a toy, pretend something, they are in a world of their own, where all their learning and developing is something that happens in passing, quite naturally, without trying.

Adults need that naturalness too. We can play. But it's the nature of being a grown-up not to spend time playing. Maybe we need to consciously do more of it. If I'm lost in play, I am being natural, like a child, not self-conscious like an adult usually is – and has to be most of the time. We lose that.

Q. What have we lost as adults that we need to get back? And what is the connection with insomnia?

A. As an ex-insomniac I have cast aside the self-consciousness of insomnia. Moving towards natural sleep is like tuning into the naturalness of childhood: letting go, being unselfconscious, in the moment, spontaneous.

When I regain naturalness things happen in passing, as by-products. It's the package deal again. When I lose myself in what I'm doing, I'm appreciating the moment, just being. I don't notice I'm enjoying myself. If I allow it – and that's not an easy thing for us adults – the natural just happens.

I can relearn that natural optimism about life, just as I could relearn natural sleep. Being closer to the natural takes time. It took practice to get back to natural sleep. And when I was there I didn't have to think about it at all.

We adults impose unnecessary limitations on ourselves most of the time. When we lose ourselves in play it helps to break down those artificial barriers. Playing is having fun, not taking things too seriously.

As an ex-insomniac I stopped taking insomnia too seriously. Insomnia, by its very nature, has a background of seriousness. But if I laughed at it, treated it as silly, this was creating a transformation like John on the beach. I lighten my mood, the opposite of getting bogged down. Of course I can't laugh at other people who are insomniacs – that's not funny. But I can laugh at myself if I choose to.

When I'm feeling down I get a bit introspective and take myself too seriously. It's better if I can make a joke of my situation. Then I'm making it my own in an empowering way. I remind myself of the introvert-extrovert spectrum – I'm not necessarily one or the other but somewhere between the two at different times. Sometimes it's possible just to switch. Ditch the glum and switch to fun. Smile to myself, change my expression on purpose – even pretend smiling has the effect of altering my mood.

Be like a child; play. Playing is using creative energy. Having fun can be a very quiet low-key thing – doing something I enjoy, any form of playing. It might be sport, music, a game, an art or craft. It's also a way of finding out about the world, just as children do. They explore and discover.

Play with words and ideas; play it by ear; be lost in play. When I'm lost in play I cast off the burden of worry about the past or the future. I am in the present enjoying myself.

It was great fun at Big Space with H. He needed me to go down the big bumpy slide with him a few times before he was confident enough to go on his own. I'd never have that opportunity otherwise. Next time I think I'll go down it anyway, even if he doesn't need me!

Be grown up in a child-like way – that sums up the ex-insomniac attitude to life. The feeling of maturing and growing in wisdom is satisfying; as is the other end of the spectrum, the feeling of being more child-like, natural.

'Play it by ear' can be a very useful phrase/concept. It means I allow myself to go forward instinctively according to present circumstances, rather than following a plan. I decide what to do as events take shape. It's a kind of improvising. That's what I'm doing in the sleep situation when I allow my body to decide. Just go with the flow. Let what happens happen without predicting or preparing for anything.

Release

Play with wording – it changes concepts. Positive, optimistic ideas can be released by playing with words. Creative energy can be there all the time but blocked, hidden behind negative phrases.

My creative energy was previously locked into insomnia. I'll just have a recap on the words I ditched, as they will be the concepts which blocked my creative energy:

My insomnia

It's out of my control

It's not my fault, it's an illness

I'm desperate to find a cure

I can hear the constriction in those words. They sound really claustrophobic. But they were ditched – words and concepts ditched in one fell swoop. I replaced the insomnia words with new words and a new mindset:

It doesn't matter if I'm awake

Leave it to my body to decide about sleep

I don't have insomnia, and it's permanent

I may not have noticed the release of creative energy at first, but I did appreciate the relief of not having insomnia in my life anymore. And what a relief the Insomnia Ditch-and-Switch was! Replacing the constricting circle with the inspiring one. Pretty amazing actually.

I still use it all the time. I want to be in the virtuous circle of confidence and control, so I make each day as relaxed as possible. I actively look for ways to take the pressure off myself. When I'm working on a task I pace myself, remembering to slow down inside whenever I can.

Feel more rested now after long sleep and relaxing day yesterday, after initial frustration with the Skoda. Went to see M's mum in Eastbourne – good to go yesterday instead of Friday so have some leeway with the Bonchurch letting, which is all underway: carpet booked, viewing times allocated (while Roger here). Embrace each thing in the present, e.g. today enjoy renovating the fireplace, knowing it's part of the schedule for letting and this is its time. Same with the Rottingdean Fair and going away to Harwich. I know what is involved in the run-up time (e.g. washing from trip, which is being done as I go along), so I can embrace Saturday (with the great satisfaction of having the Anthology to sell) and enjoy the Harwich trip when it's time for that.

I released myself from the horrible circle of stress and insomnia and I will never go back to it. This certainty gives me a sense of self, a feeling of my individuality and my own expertise. It's up to me, of course, what I regard as creativity and what I value as my expertise. I am proud of the research I have done on myself to become an ex-insomniac. It leads to confidence, then to exploring and being creative.

Switching circles is liberating, energising. Mind flexibility engenders more of itself. My repertoire of tools enables and empowers me to be creative and self-reliant. I feel another mission statement coming on:

I will keep the idea of released creative energy and use it. I will look out for opportunities to make things interesting and enjoyable.

It's Poems Out Loud this morning (even though it's a bank

holiday) and that's a good antidote to all the work over the weekend. It's good to find a creative activity for myself, something which injects fun or interest into my busy life. I know it's an important element in my life – not just a distraction which can be left out if I don't feel like it or I'm too busy to be bothered with it.

'Make it interesting' has become a mantra of mine – I've used it in lots of situations. I made insomnia interesting, didn't I? Against all the odds. So I can find interest in other difficult and uncomfortable situations.

There are issues cropping up all the time where I think the secret is to make things interesting for myself. I found myself doing that with tinnitus – being interested in the sounds in my ear, rather than being afraid of unwanted noise. I was doing the same thing as I'd done with insomnia. Seeing myself as an interesting case study!

The ex-insomniac way has real strength. I benefit more and more from the creative energy released by the Insomnia Ditch-and-Switch. I often find myself exploring and being curious.

Yesterday was interesting – I needed to be very flexible about my day – reassessing as I went along. It started with disruption to trains making London non-viable. So I followed my nose and amazingly ended up sitting in a church listening to a wonderful concert. I heard nearly all of an hour-long lunch-time performance – piano and soprano. I'd intended stopping in Seaford for lunch – found an unusual little café down from the seafront, then wandered across to St Leonard's church where I happened upon the concert. After that I strolled along the promenade with a hot chocolate, making for the Martello tower – but I was not so lucky there – museum's still shut even though I was there for the stated opening times. No problem – that was part of following my nose/ playing it by ear.

12
Life and story

Our own narrative

"Is everything alright?" both the adult and the child inside me asks. Everyone has the need to feel safe and not be frightened in the world. But we live with positive and negative forces within ourselves and in relation to others.

Everyone's perception of threat is different, yet we're all in the same boat. We seek freedom and fulfilment in life, but we all have inner struggle – none of us can avoid fears and insecurities. We want to be alright within ourselves, to feel secure in our own company. We relate to others so as not to feel or be alone.

I remember when I was a chronic insomniac how much I needed other people to know the extent of my suffering and to empathise.

Often it backfired, though. They could say such frustrating things: "But you probably *have* slept". I would bristle silently at that: "I know I haven't. I'm not lying. Can't you just believe me?"

People who'd never had insomnia seemed to have plenty to say about it. They gave me their thoughts and suggestions, even though they had no idea what chronic insomnia was like, and didn't want to find out by asking me. No doubt they meant well, but I remember it being very annoying. One person mixed it up with the odd time she'd been up and about in the middle of the night. "Oh, I think insomnia is wonderful. I find it so enjoyable and a little bit exciting, too, in a way." Yes I remember that. It made me mad, what they said, how little they knew. I wanted to ignore them but I couldn't help being emotionally affected. The unguarded trivialising cut right into me.

I mentioned just in passing the claims for lavender products from the website I'd seen, thinking they were laughable. But several people in the group thought they sounded good and worth trying. It came back to me how little most people understand about how difficult insomnia is/ how far from sleep an insomniac is/ how ridiculous this typical suggestion of a cure is. And I remembered how frustrated I used to get.

It is frustrating – relating to others feels like such a hit-and-miss thing. We each have our own different perceptions yet need so much to identify with others. It's not easy – a source of much stress. Not surprising when you think of it – how we are grappling with fundamental human issues as we strive to find our place in the world and feel at ease in it. Of course we need to communicate one human being to another.

That's why we so naturally tell and hear stories. We listen and learn from other people's stories and we want others to hear ours. We like hearing about others' lives, however trivial an anecdote might be.

Story in all its forms is a powerful tool for communication

with others. We need it as an antidote for potential confusion and fear – though, as we know, stories (other people's or even our own) are not always reliable.

Memory too provides an incomplete and unreliable story. No matter how clearly I think I've remembered something, my brain will have been adjusting, compensating, rearranging – all manner of behind-the-scenes activities.

Q. But it is possible to have some mastery over it, isn't it?

A. Yes, I can steer myself away from a rigid and potentially misleading narrative of events. I just need to be aware that my memory can deceive me. I need to have an open mind about remembered things.

Mind flexibility makes a big difference to communication – and to stress. I think it's about trying not to create a fixed narrative of events in my mind. I know we all do it. But, if I think about it, a situation I worry about at one point in time is very unlikely to stay the same. That's because there are other people and aspects to it that I will not be aware of. It helps to take this into account when I'm stressing about an event or about what someone's said or done. Things will already have changed and moved on, most likely without reference to me at all.

It's actually quite liberating to recognise that mine is not the only and correct reading of a situation. When I recognise my picture is only one tiny aspect of the whole, it helps to stop the stress. It takes the pressure off and pre-empts frustration.

Along with that, I stop assuming I was correct about other

people's feelings and thinking on the subject. Then I can begin to tackle my own stress reactions. Instead of being held back, led up the garden path by false assumptions, I can move forward. I empower myself that way.

The opposite of empowerment is strikingly illustrated in a Maupassant story, The Necklace. It is about excruciating frustration. A couple spend years in penury, working to repay a debt; the diamond necklace they had borrowed was stolen and had to be replaced. It was all unnecessary, as the necklace was a fake.

The extreme-case scenario in that story is very useful for feedback – how not to be. The Maupassant characters were victims. They spent a whole lifetime of stress, not recognising the 'picture' was different from how they'd assumed it to be.

It was all so interesting yesterday – the way it went with the issue of the website images. It brought to mind the Maupassant story of the Necklace – J on holiday in Romania scouring Bucharest for an internet café when the images were related to something else, not urgent at all! I laughed at myself when the 'dénouement' came – a fuss about nothing.

But at the time it was real and discomfiting, and potentially very frustrating, seeing that it was all unnecessary. Laughing at myself and the situation, when it had unravelled, stopped any frustration. And because it was amusing it was ripe for feedback and learning for next time.

My insight is: I'm afraid of frustration. It's an emotion that affects me quite strongly. I sense when something is likely to cause me frustration and my nerves kick in. As an ex-insomniac I recognise it and have strategies. Yesterday it was the one practical idea (I texted for an update) which set in motion the disentangling. The problem melted away.

By the way I did acknowledge the episode was far more frustrating for J and Sophia than it was for me! But I expect they had a laugh about it at some point.

My evolving story

"How long does it take?" All insomniacs want quick fixes. "Just tell me how I can get to sleep. And if I wake up, tell me how I can get back to sleep again." That's all you need to know. End of story. (The end of insomnia: 1)

I was like that – stuck in the vicious insomnia circle. But I ditched it – switched to the confidence-and-control sort.

Then a new story began. A story with a completely different feel to it.

It wasn't about my struggle to achieve an end result. I no longer had the definite goal of being free of insomnia. It became more natural than that – the idea of a continuous path emerged, a continuum. I was moving forwards seeing where my ex-insomniac mindset would take me – my own post-insomnia story evolving. It twists and turns and changes. It has analogies like mini stories within it.

I used my new mindset on insomnia to help with other challenges. Or was it that other challenges – working on myself in a way – helped me with insomnia? I'm not sure which way round it was. It was all inter-related and organic.

It was just like that with skiing and insomnia. I had a feeling these two stories of mine were connected, so I put some of my skiing milestones into a mini story for you:

Fear and Challenge
(by an Ex-Insomniac)

Obstacle course

(Loudspeaker) 'And next up we have Nicki Gillard from England.'

"Maarten, how do I make this first turn?"

"Just go, Nicki."

(Loudspeaker) 'Ready, Nicki. Three, two, one, go!'

Slalom's done. I'm on the straight steep bit.

"Stop, Nicki! Wait! Go back!" I hear my team-mates shouting.

Whoops, I've forgotten the schnapps. The lady comes running up behind me. I swig it and off.

Grab the ball and throw it in the toad's mouth – missed. Try again. "No, Nicki, leave it!" they all scream.

Next the narrow passage under the big bunny's legs. I'm through and out the other side.

Duck down. It's the low-pole limbo. I did it.

Ski fast now to the finish. Yes!

"It's a shame you lost time on the schnapps, Nicki, but don't worry. You finished, that's the main thing. We'll get loads of team points for that."

Worried about points – you're joking! I'm ecstatic, elated, on cloud nine.

I was that proud of myself I carried a picture of Big Bunny with me for months afterwards. (It was my mobile-phone wallpaper.)

* * *

Giving up skiing

I've been standing here for about half an hour watching people come up on the lift. They look down at the slope and ski off. I've seen the same ones go down and come up again several times now. But I'm stuck. It's not that I'm nervous. I travelled here to Milton Keynes Snozone by myself, got my skis, put on my boots, went up the drag-lift, all done with nerves well under control. So why don't I just ski off like everyone else? I can ski, can't I? I've skied through the bunny's legs for goodness sake. It's just that I never really understood how to turn. I'm a slalom champion who doesn't know how to turn. How paradoxical is that? There is no other way down, so I'll just have to go.

I tried to turn but it didn't work. I've got myself to the side and people are skiing past me. Someone's helped me up and I can ski down the rest of the slope no problem. But I realise I've hurt my leg.

It was quite painful driving back, but I didn't know until I had my massage with Jane a few days later that my left calf muscle had been badly torn.

Diary entry: It's my choice not to carry on with the skiing but to look at other options. It's a positive way forward – liberating – not stuck in the past, bogged down by unachievable goals based on what other people do, rather than what is right for me. It's an important episode in my life really – it has taught me a lot and I've reached a good point with regard to personal challenge.

* * *

Back at the Snozone

One year later

I used my mantra 'really wide snow plough' and concentrated on the ground immediately beneath me, not thinking ahead even so far as the first turn. I know I'm safe with that really wide plough, so no need to consider turning – it's up to me – or up to my body actually. It just happens. I don't need to think at all. Now I feel I've made it my own – there's no set way to get down the slope, I can please myself – it's lovely. The snow plough ironically is my friend now (I used to think it held me back) – just for now anyway, while I need it. I can see I won't need it much longer for the turns, as the parallel feels as though it's taking over. I'll just observe that next time.

Q. So what happened the time before?

A. I hadn't given my body the chance to get into its stride. I'd gone straight up to the top, assuming it would all just happen, when really I was rehearsing the actions required in my head. My poor body was the innocent victim and sustained a muscle injury as a result.

* * *

No poles

I let it happen this time and observed what my body was doing when allowed to take over. Yesterday I enjoyed it. I practised what I was comfortable with and didn't think about the technical points. I just skied and noticed where I was transferring my weight, edging in, naturally standing up and bending lower. There was just a point when my body went into the rhythm of the turn. It was much better without poles – found my natural balance

It marked a big difference in my attitude to skiing and my feel for it. I'd made the basics my own and they are not just for the beginning; they underpin the whole continuum.

I feel I'm on the continuum now – a very good feeling of calm satisfaction. It has been there all along – my body knows what it wants to do but my head has been pulling it around, stifling its natural flow.

* * *

I'm in control

While the others went off all around the reds and blacks I found a lovely nursery slope. I made it my own, going up and down the drag lift and getting into the flow of the skiing, enjoying myself. This was new.

I missed all of that when we got home; I wanted to be there, not leave it behind. I wanted to hold on to the pleasure of it. So I watched videos on skiing technique, as J had suggested but I never wanted to before. Now I wanted to see where that continuum was leading. I heard what the instructor Darren Turner was saying on the video and instantly related to it: "You'll always speed up when you start the turn – you can't change that. But what you can change is how fast you're going before that, and then start the next turn feeling a lot calmer, less stressed, and happier about life." Then I realised he was using words like 'confidence and control'. "Now where have I heard that before?" I was on a roll so I noted down some other things the instructor said: Make it easier for yourself; practice makes permanent; it will start to become natural; because I'm in control I don't need to rush into the turn. "It's uncanny how connected it all is with my ex-insomniac stuff," I thought. And what about this: analogies! 'Skis are like the clutch and accelerator when you drive; make a smooth turn on your skis like you lean into a corner smoothly on your bike.' And I realised with immense satisfaction it was true: everybody does love an analogy.

* * *

Before: Skiing as an insomniac

I'm hurtling down the slope overtaking everyone. My speed is breath-taking. And that's just me lying awake reliving it. Over and over – it won't go away. The adrenalin rush is now a permanent fixture. At breakfast the next morning everyone is preparing for the day's skiing but I'm an insomnia wreck. "I just don't want snow in my life!" I say. Everyone laughs. But I'm only half joking. I couldn't sleep because of the skiing and I couldn't ski after not sleeping all night. How funny is that?

* * *

Later on: Skiing as an ex-insomniac

Looking back, did insomnia help me with skiing or did skiing help me with insomnia? I don't know which way round it was and it doesn't matter. I just like the story of it and where I am now.

Part Four
For life's ups and downs

I have needed to call upon my ex-insomniac mindset very much over the last three or four years.

M's stress built up and turned into a (late-) mid-life crisis. His actions and behaviour threw off balance the basic levelness of our lives, knocking our marriage sideways. But I will not blame him. Mental illness is not a person's fault.

The last part focuses on life's ups and downs and personal highs and lows. The Insomnia Ditch-and-Switch and the mindset behind it go on working and helping.

13
Positive about Uncertainty

Our own reference points

At every stage of our lives from early childhood onwards we human beings are trying to make sense of the world around us. Not only that; we are trying to find our own place in it. The more we learn to do all that the trickier it becomes and the more we have to struggle to overcome difficulties. We learn to fit into the world according to our own parameters. But we must do all this while relating to other people at the same time. No easy task.

It's not surprising that at times our world feels like a very uncertain place. We know there are no absolute certainties in life; that the only certain thing is change. But sometimes we have a need to stop things changing, when we get that out-of-control feeling. Then we try to seize hold of certainties.

It was like that when I was in the grip of insomnia. Fear of not sleeping meshed in with fear of losing control. It was a horrible feeling. I became more and more desperate to regain control. I wanted somebody or something to guarantee the outcome I desired.

But being desperate for a certain outcome ("I must sleep") got me nowhere. It brought only more anxiety. What actually freed me up was ditching all that. Ditching that whole mindset. I took control in a practical way, letting go and allowing my body to decide about sleep. I became permanently free of insomnia because I was no longer dependent on an external result. I could rely on myself, on my own mindset. How liberating was that!

Ditching brought a wonderful breath of fresh air. But my fears took a while to un-bed. I'd ditched the security blanket of carefully honed routines and that was scary. All my insomniac dos and don'ts were a trap, but for a long time they had been essential. They promised security, control – above all a return to normal sleep. When I feared normality slipping away, the desire for it was very strong. But what is normal?

Q. Is there such a thing as a normal sleep pattern?

A. I don't believe there is.

For me it's unhelpful to think in terms of normal sleep, just as it was unhelpful to think in terms of a cure for insomnia. Trying to force some version of normality on myself is a hiding to nowhere. It would be stressful and pointless. The liberating way is to use my own reference points. Sleep is an individual thing. It's about what feels okay to me.

And I find it better not to think in terms of a pattern at all. 'Pattern' feels like a restricting word. I'd like to ditch that too. I prefer not to have any fixed external idea about how long a person should sleep or how to judge my quality of sleep, but to decide for myself. I much prefer my ex-insomniac approach.

No result required

When I was an insomniac the stress and fear of being awake fed off my anxious desire to get to sleep. But, once I allowed my body to decide, sleep happened naturally.

Tuning in to the natural is about allowing first, letting go and freeing myself, instead of remaining stuck. It happens when I accept I'm not sleeping and do this without making judgments or blaming, allowing my body to decide, letting it be.

It's not easy to let it be. My default reaction is to demand results – and as instantly as possible. "Sounds like panicking", an ex-insomniac might say to that. "Instead, trust yourself enough to let go of your security blanket – go without the water-tight plan and be alright anyway."

Q. Security blanket – the one you clutch in a bid for certainty and control?

A. Yes, that's right.

Q. Water-tight plan?

A. The plan that isn't water-tight at all. It's really a hope and a prayer for a result and, as we know, it's totally counter-productive.

An ex-insomniac again (who has ditched the desperation): "Some things you can't control and some you can. Allow uncertainty. Let it be."

It seems to have become a mantra of mine – no result required. It reminds me to allow things to happen naturally sometimes, when I might otherwise be trying too hard to achieve a particular outcome.

It's about relaxing enough to play it by ear. Not knowing the outcome can be exciting (with a tinge of scary). There can be joy in the uncertain nature of the world. Another way of looking at uncertainty is spontaneity – interesting things happening unplanned and unexpected.

No result or outcome was required for insomnia. And it was just the same with tinnitus – no result required with that either. I wasn't trying to get rid of the sounds (though I did ditch the word/concept of tinnitus). And interestingly, I thought, it's the same with H's toddler talk. There's no aim that he should say certain words or learn speech in a set way. He's picking up language as he goes along, communicating with people around him – and with himself.

With expansive open-ended things like language acquisition the sky is the limit, meaning there's no limit. There's no end result, no direct aim. Like a Zen archer, aiming at a target would get in the way. It would seriously spoil the flow.

Trying to sleep doesn't work. Having sleep as a target seriously spoils the flow. Natural sleep happens when I let go of the target. I don't notice when I fall asleep. I take sleep for granted and I don't bother about it.

My friend's son recently conquered his fear of flying. I asked her how he felt about it now. "He took it in his stride," she said.

After all, when you're flying in a plane you just sit there, don't you?

But as she still has her own fear of flying she doesn't quite see it like that.

Q. What does it feel like when you've ditched insomnia?

A. Maybe quiet satisfaction at first, but then there's nothing to feel anything about. You just sleep when you sleep, don't you?

And now, when I think about my fear of snorkelling, I wonder what all the fuss was about. You just float really, don't you?

I'm nearly there with the skiing. I know what I'll say: What was all the fuss about? You just let the snow slide under you.

Tackle my own reactions

Having my own reference points; letting go of trying to get a result; allowing the natural: all these things help me deal with fears and feelings of uncertainty in day-to-day living.

Q. How?

A. It's all about having practical strategies

I can use my ex-insomniac tools and strategies to help me adjust my mood during the day. I'm used to doing research on myself and giving myself feedback – handling my relationship with myself, you could say.

You may be interested in this dream I had. I wrote about it in my diary, about how it affected my mood during the day and what advice I gave to myself.

The dream I had unnerved me yesterday just before waking. Sand – piles of it – where did that come from?? A deep pit – the sand came down on top of me – I did it to myself, almost casually. It gave me an underlying mild anxiety through the day. I knew it was only the situation from my dream, not a real feeling at all, not a reaction to an actual event. Obviously it referred to something, but there is no way of knowing exactly what. I could think back to what the feeling was, though: a fear of bringing the whole lot down on my head. Doing it to myself was a big element in the dream – being the cause (quite unnecessarily too – in an almost blasé way) of my own destruction. It was a very dramatic scenario. It suggests a real sense of foreboding, and a fear I must have – it felt like a window on my psyche! Also I think I'll know as time goes by what it refers to, because the fear will come more into focus. If not, it can't have been important. I won't make a big thing of it anyway – only as far as it's interesting and helpful; obviously nothing spooky, only rational.

There's no point in speculating on the whys and wherefores – just as I don't do causes and triggers when I'm awake in the night.

Address my present mood, and use strategies to alter it. So it's:

> Ditch the complexities and complications. Clear the decks.

> Then ditch the emotion and switch to the practical. Get my practical voice.
>
> Think of one practical thing I can do now to make myself feel better.

And later on, after following my own advice –

While I was walking up the hill, I worked out what it was in my dream. It was about frustration. I could not have worked it all out before I'd adjusted my mood. I had to be feeling more positive and business-like to go up the hill in the first place. I generalised about how frustration, or fear of it, has affected me in the past and is affecting me now. And I realised I shouldn't heed those sensations. Instead, I should regard them as temporary physiological reactions to a vague generalised fear. Nothing to concern myself about at all

Fear of frustration; everyone finds sometimes they're in a disempowering situation. Not having control can be very stressful. Like everyone, I get these annoying situations cropping up. They go straight to my vulnerable point. I go from resilient to stressed in an instant, as though my human frailty has suddenly been exposed.

My struggles and discoveries post insomnia have taken me some way towards forming a practical strategy for dealing with the stresses and worries that come along.

Now I try to find empowerment in potentially frustrating situations. Do something. Find something – on purpose. Go straight into the potentially frustrating situation with eyes wide open. The fear is I'll bring everything crashing down on top of me (dream symbolism) but probably not in fact.

The website issue was one small instance of it. As predicted, when I faced it out (gently, not all guns blazing) and asked first Trev then Sarah about the invoice, it unravelled itself. The frustration of not getting my point across is the bug-bear for me. I think it causes me quite a lot of stress. When I think back to times that were particularly frustrating in my life, it's often to do with being unfairly treated in some way and not being able to speak out about it.

I realise now that, when I'm confident, I don't have to go making my point all the time. I can keep my viewpoint in the wings while I listen to what the other person has to say on the matter. I might change my mind anyway, or adapt my view. I don't know until I get into it. I haven't avoided it, that's the important thing. I can bide my time and make my point as and when – that takes confidence and control. It's the virtuous circle.

I can balance the need to get my point across with listening to the other person and letting them get their point across, so they won't be frustrated. Shifting my perspective takes quite some presence of mind, but it's worth it.

Then I am generous-spirited. Being fearful of frustration and pre-empting a frustrating conversation – false anticipation probably – makes me angry and mean-spirited. 'Mellow' is a useful word here, not angry anymore (and potential frustration is akin to anger). It's the ex-insomniac way of being and acting, using balance. It goes something like this: "I will go directly into it unabashed and unafraid, but gently and mildly in action."

It's not easy to shift that frustration; it's my fear. Fear of frustration. Some people have fear of anxiety or fear of feeling guilty. This fear of mine will have been there a long time in one guise or another. It will come back and it will have to be ditched again.

Didn't hear from J – obviously they're not thinking about website graphics when they're enjoying their trip. I tried doing 'why does it matter to me?' which does work to some extent. It's important to me to get over this. There are lots of similar times – it's being dependent on someone else to do a job, when you feel the weight of responsibility. So it's a disempowered feeling; it's frustrating not to be able to take control and do something about it yourself. I could at least text J and ask for an update. Yes, that's one practical thing to do. Good, I feel better already. Then I'll start my day.

Sometimes it's therapeutic to laugh at my own reactions. It creates feedback I can use in my virtuous circle. That's different from self-mocking. I'm laughing with myself in a way, not at myself. You know when someone laughs at you in a mocking way, not with you. It has a totally different feel – not enjoyment, but criticism implied. This sort is positive and empowering.

The issue still feels annoying but without the underlying frustration; so the wording should be different now: instead of 'issue', actually no wording at all! That's interesting too. Let it drop. The issue evaporated as it unravelled. It has dropped itself. It was only there as an issue in my mind – I'd made too much of it, putting it together like a story with characters and events playing parts in it. Silly really but interesting – it's what we do

'Let it drop' is a useful expression. It's about allowing. Allow the issue to unravel all by itself. It's often what has to be done with a load of things. 'Load' is useful there too. These issues are heavy and a burden.

We have broad anxieties (it's the human condition), as well as day-to-day worries and annoyances. It's impossible to work it all out, to find out what's behind it all, or to disentangle all the threads. To imagine someone accurately doing that would be to grossly over-simplify.

But what I can do is tackle my own reactions in the best way I can. I have practical strategies for that. I will start as I mean to go on, be proactive. I will motivate myself to start a process and see it through – not to the point of a goal, but as an ongoing approach to living.

Know you're covered

I'm waking up and immediately waiting for an issue to come into my head. Which one will it be? I do a bit of a scan to see if everything's alright, but with an underlying misgiving. Then it's as though one of them has to jump into the gap. Catch hold of it and ward it off. I'm covering myself. I'm trying to guard myself against stress.

Yes, it's completely understandable to try and ward off difficult things. Isn't it sensible to take avoidance action?

The only thing is – it doesn't work. If the worrying issue is hidden, it can't be dealt with. The worry stays vague and insidious, incubating stress. Covering myself against stress turns out to be stress-inducing. Any sense of security it may give me is false.

I know this from my experience with insomnia; mirrored in snorkelling and skiing; and confirmed in different situations life has conjured up. Sometimes the safe positions I construct for myself are not safe at all. Quite the opposite. I know, too, that the ex-insomniac mindset is about giving myself real positions of safety, sustainable ones.

So this safety thing can go two ways, positive or negative. Are you expecting a table now? Then I won't disappoint you:

Safe: positive	Safe: negative
Safety net	Security blanket
'Everything's alright' mantra	Hide in my comfort zone
I'm covered: play it by ear	I'm covering myself: keep the water-tight plan
Take on challenges	Avoid challenging situations
Observe my nerviness	Guard against nerves
Practical response	Emotional response
Moving forward	Retreating
Let go	Resist

Taking control	Being controlled
Bring fear into the open	Push fear away

These, on both sides, are safe fall-back positions, but one side has self-motivation behind it, the other has retracting. One I associate with being an ex-insomniac, the other with insomnia. It's the difference between having a feeling you can bask in or feeling unnerved and insecure in an endless chain of fear. I'm not exaggerating.

I knew all about negative what-ifs when I was afraid of snorkelling. How different it was when I'd faced my fear of it! I could let go and relax in the moment.

(Snorkelling: 9) I know what I used to be like: Where am I going to get out of the water? What exactly will I do? What if there's a problem? That's the big unhelpful mode of thinking: what if….Therein lies an endless chain of fear – when I race ahead in my thoughts. But I can stop it now – on the first level of the scale – easy. I recognise each particular 'what if' and don't bother with it. Instead I go back to the moment. I know I'm covered. I can bask in this feeling of being okay.

Taming fear

At first I didn't see insomnia as a fear to be faced. I had to identify it, recognise it as fear, and then I could face it. I could ditch the fear and the insomnia for good.

At the weekend in the park with the children I happened to be in a scenario all about this. H and I found ourselves having to face our fear, and we bravely stood up to Daddy Monster:

> *When normally nice Nana turns into Na-na Ro-bot, Na-na Ro-bot, her eyes go stary, her legs go stiff, her arms go threatening, her fingers claw like a witch's.*
>
> *And Henry can do it too. He knows how to turn into Na-na Ro-bot himself. He's got the legs, the arms, the fingers, and the voice. As instant as Na-na herself does it.*
>
> *We're both going, Na-na Ro-bot, Na-na Ro-bot, really scary.*
>
> *In the very same instant Daddy Monster changes too. He's the one who's scared now.*
>
> *We're chasing the monster.*
>
> *We're scaring the monster.*
>
> *It's immensely satisfying, I can tell you.*

With insomnia I faced my fear. I identified it and stood up to it. I put myself in charge – I would not be at its mercy. It was brave of me to do that. And I liked being brave. I infinitely preferred it to cowering under insomnia's power.

But what if those insidious, vague fears come on their own with no tangible context? In a way it's easier if you've got something obvious to fight against, like insomnia. But vague fears hover in the background, accompanied by a lurking fear of potential fear. Horrible.

Q. What do you do if you can't identify your fear?

A. I leave it to my body.

Trust my body to deal with the sensations. Like nerves, keep these vague fears where I can see them. Focus on them. Be in the moment with them.

This time, when I was skiing and feeling very nervous at the top of a slope, I dealt with the nerves themselves. I knew it wasn't really fear of skiing, because I had my 'really wide snow plough' mantra to cover myself. I've been dealing with nerves pretty efficiently for quite a while now (post insomnia), so it was second nature to me. Anyway I didn't need to go into the plough as it turned out; it just gave me confidence. So I did just ski off.

The really wide snow plough was my safety-net mantra. It clarified and simplified things as a background no-doubt mindset. A firm footing – no need to think about it – an instant clear positive message to my brain. I have my grounding base position. From there I can move forward on instinct, playing it by ear, anxiety-free, because I have that positive fall-back in place.

I thought of another way of saying leave it to my body: delegate. It's a kind of allowing. Let my body deal with sensations.

It works for the butterflies I get when I'm anxious. It works for stress. It works for difficult and confusing feelings. It's about my mind allowing my body to work for me.

Q. How do you let your body deal with butterflies in your stomach?

A. Focus on them, observe them, notice exactly what they're like. They are what they are, no more, no less.

But my mind says, "I've got butterflies in my stomach. That means I'm really nervous about something." So my thoughts go racing ahead, "Oh no, what if this, what if that?" My mind sets off a chain reaction of links, and the vicious circle gets into full flow really fast.

That is how my mind deals with the butterflies. Not great. My body's way is quite a bit better, don't you think? "Okay, they are right here in the pit of my stomach; this is what they're like. Let's just stick with them."

My body wants to do its job, processing sensations. It is the kind of task it likes to be given.

And it's great to have this bodily manifestation of something intangible like fear. Bodily means tangible, because I can locate it, feel it, observe it, keep it where I can see it.

I'll cast my mind back for a moment to that horrible scenario – pushing the pram along the South Coast Road, unable to go home: I don't have the patience to stop and turn. The butterflies won't allow it. I'm at their mercy. (Tyranny of time: 7)

I'm not at their mercy now. I tamed the butterflies, so they are no longer a threat to me. I can deal with them any time they come my way. I'll delegate them to my body.

I delegated sleep to my body. I tamed my fear of not sleeping. I don't have it anymore.

In a challenging situation

Q. Some fears are so difficult to face, you can only contemplate avoidance. What do you do then?

A. In a case like that – my own experience tells me – I need an analogy. Did I mention we all need (and love) analogies? I'll think of a fearful situation or struggle I overcame.

Okay, for me, it's skiing. I overcame it like this: I had the presence of mind not to think about my fear in advance; I waited and when the time came I let my body deal with it. I tackled my fear by dealing with the sensation of it in the present moment.

I know I can only successfully deal with fear in the present. Fear is felt in the present. The problem is thinking of a block of fear associated with the past and future, not the detailed actual and real feeling. I know this.

Yes, that's exactly how I overcame my fear of skiing and I can repeat the same kind of experience. If I want to, that is. The important thing is it's entirely up to me. If I want to, I can go into it with my eyes wide open and the will to overcome even a long-standing fear (maybe bordering on a phobia).

Q. What if a difficult situation takes you unawares?

A. Then I'll be equipped to deal with that, whatever it is.

A difficult situation took me unawares a couple of months ago and, yes, I reckon I was equipped to deal with it. Here's what happened —

Do you remember the paradox of the slalom champion who didn't know how to turn? Well, this is the case of the author who didn't know how to write.

Everyone's sitting round a very long rectangular pine table, informal boardroom-style. I'm ready, confident, pen poised. The tutor explains the exercise – he's previously handed out pictures on postcards, each one unusual. We must imagine this depicts a page in the middle of a novel, so start dot, dot, dot. Everyone's pen hits the paper – sounds of flowing words, a page of foolscap covered in a trice (just as well, we only have 10 minutes). But me – wait, hold on, I can't think of anything to write, everything that comes into my head sounds stupid. I can't even start. But I must. I should've written loads by now, time's nearly up. I put something down – a few ideas, question form, nothing flowing. Not like the others. Time to go round the table reading out our work. Round we go. Mine amongst them – short and confident (that's the trick). It came out short and stupid. Obviously someone who doesn't know how to write. This felt very confusing and really quite unpleasant. Over several days of the course the format didn't change and neither did my flow.

Q. How did you do in that difficult and challenging situation? Did you keep your nerve?

A. Yes, I did – I was alright at the time. I had my body to tune into, steadying me in the moment. So I can say I was equipped to deal with it.

I was alright in each present moment. That held me in good stead. What would have been an ordeal became a learning experience. I'm proud of myself for that. It was very interesting reading my diary before the trip – I could not have envisaged the exact nature of the experience and how horrible it would be. But the advice I gave to myself then applies just as much now: there are lots of ways the experience might help me move forward.

Q. What advice did you give to yourself?

A. As soon as I could, I stopped looking back and assessing things in a nervy, emotional way. There has to be some looking back, of course, but I'm better when I start to think proactively: gain valuable feedback to inform my thinking.

That's part of processing the emotions. It's been helpful sharing it with different people too. I know I'll be able to use the experience itself and my dealing with it. Find it interesting, that's the thing.

Q. How will you use this?

A. I don't have to worry in advance; or look back and worry. What happened/what I did/how I reacted – it is what it is. I can't change that. And there's no need to worry that I can't. I am, and was, alright in each present moment – and I can move forward positively with that knowledge. That will always be the case.

Author's note: By the way, in the end I proved I could write. At the final readings evening my story 'The Passenger' was well received. I didn't write it there, but I reworked it from what I'd learnt on the course. I was satisfied with that.

14
Equilibrium

Relaxed mindset

Insomnia binds you to the past and future – it perniciously focuses your mind on 'I haven't fallen asleep yet. What if I don't sleep? What will I be like in the morning?' and so on.

Peace of mind is in the present: 'I don't mind being awake'.

Q. But what if you do mind being awake?

A. Select a different mantra.

For example, in the situation of young children disturbing my sleep: I accept being awake. I'm not going to get stressed about the circumstances. Not sleeping won't do me harm.

Or if I'm awake ruminating over relationship issues: I won't do this thinking lying in bed. I know that's counter-productive. It's a great help to know: it doesn't matter if I'm not sleeping right now.

I can always say to myself: okay I'm awake but my body will take care of sleeping when the time comes, so I don't need to interfere. I don't need to have an opinion about it. Being awake isn't an issue when I know that. This is what 'I don't have insomnia' means – being awake is not insomnia. My role is to rest and leave sleep to my body. This is a very reassuring thing.

Times like this where I'm struggling are learning opportunities. If I really internalise the idea of sleep not being an issue, bit by bit, practising, it will become second nature. I'm still learning it. It's counter-intuitive. But I can feel it sinking in – it's the evidence that counts.

There's still an edge of stress, which seems to hover and abate. I know I'm touchy and resilient in equal measure – but it's understandable and I can deal with it. Having a good attitude to sleep is crucial: more 'it doesn't matter if I'm awake' last night, rather than 'I don't mind being awake', because I did mind! But it didn't matter, that was the point, and my tired explanation to myself (about alcohol and adrenalin) dissipated when I selected the right mantra. That's something important actually – selecting one that's appropriate at the time – tailoring.

Just be – allow my body to decide about sleep. That's the relaxed mindset, the quiet satisfaction that comes from the virtuous circle of confidence and control.

Q. But what if you still feel awful the next morning?

A. That happens. Allow it.

I'm writing this on the train, feeling awful. I was awake for a long time in the night and had to get up when I wasn't ready. This is my own advice to myself:

In the night resting is an important element to go with 'it doesn't matter if I'm awake'.

In the morning look forward as soon as possible (it's natural to look back at first)

Put it behind me, by leaning on my ex-insomniac mindset/practice. Be in the moment as I get up. I will be fine bodily, remember that and feel it by tuning in to my body (just as I did with nerves – keeping them where I can see them)

Directly locate my bodily sensations of waking/ getting up too soon, the effects on me of not sleeping as much as I think I needed.

The generalised spaced-out feeling – where exactly is it? Give details. For me now: top of my nose, eyes, top lip, my breathing – the breath feels hotter. But I won't interpret that as an ill feeling (raised temperature).

Compare this to my insomniac's description of the physical results of a sleepless night (illness taking over my head and my whole body). This current one is not negative, just factual and objective. I know I'm alright now and will be, going forward. I don't feel great but why worry? It's not permanent and it won't sap my energy.

There's an energy based on confidence and control, a mindset energy (connected with creative energy). It can be low-key. It's another form of confidence. (See list below)

The key is not to let thoughts get mixed in with these bodily sensations. No need to be low in mood because of them. Don't allow false/unhelpful associations. (How I'm feeling has nothing to do with M.) Stop the link on purpose, so my mood is not unnecessarily/artificially lowered by having time awake in the night – I can deal with the physiological sensations on their own/in their own right.

Doesn't mean I have to be full of the joys of spring – just not low. I don't have to feel marvellous. Okay will do. It won't stop me enjoying things spontaneously as I go about my day. Not if my mood isn't low. And why should it be? I can feel rough without being low in spirits if I appreciate/allow/am aware of the difference.

Go easy on myself. I can rest inside even when I'm busy during the day, slowing for a while on purpose. Resting inside – taking a moment to just be. Peace of mind is in the present. Reassure myself – I'm alright here and now.

What a difference before and after, insomniac and ex-insomniac!

Before, this would have been considered a relapse of insomnia. Next morning the physical feel of it would have been the same (in kind, though not in intensity) but the mindset completely different. And so too my sleep the following night.

My attitude changed everything about the next day as well as the night. Now the glass is half full. I had an appreciation of the sleep time (as and when my body was ready for sleep) and the resting time too.

I relaxed into that mindset as I continued my day.

Energy and focus

I mentioned the list I made on the train – a list of different forms of confidence. I wanted to confirm my basic motivation to be positive about the day, even though at the time I was feeling pretty awful. This is what I wrote down:

Forms of confidence:

> *Energy (body)*
>
> *Energy (mind)*
>
> *Optimism (half-full/half-empty) positivity*
>
> *Appreciation of the present – tuning in:*
>
> *Creative mindset*
>
> *Self-confidence – trusting myself*
>
> *Motivation (spark)*

Q. What is this spark?

A. My spark is my motivation.

It comes from my ex-insomniac mindset, and it has given me more and more energy in different guises.

Getting more energy can mean slowing things down. Sometimes less is more. I slow down instead of rushing and I accomplish more.

Post insomnia, resting inside is an essential part of my attitude, especially when I've not had enough sleep in the night. It's how I retain my energy for the day ahead – a way of pacing myself.

Now I slow my pace on purpose whenever I remember to do it. That might not mean taking longer. Two minutes on an electric toothbrush with a slowed-down brushing motion still takes two minutes! When I'm chewing gum I always seem to do it really fast until I deliberately slow it down. It works like magic on my composure.

It's about paying attention to what I'm doing, giving each thing more focus. I did that when I was studying myself as I was awake in the night. Finding it interesting.

I stop racing ahead inside and – it happens in an instant – creative energy takes the place of nervous energy. I allow myself time to appreciate the qualities, the detail, the intrinsic beauty or interestingness of things. It's about being in the moment. It is creative focus.

J and I chatted about the weather and how one should embrace grey skies, autumnal wind and rain, just as worthy of appreciation as a pink glow or crisp sun on autumn colours. How great when drizzle is a pleasurable experience!

As I mentioned, my job after teaching became property maintenance and letting. I find the ex-insomniac approach really helps me in my work. Just being and tuning in – I think I was doing this the other day:

Nice productive day. I like being efficient with a business-like but relaxed manner. It's about being in the moment while I'm getting jobs done that require an overview of what's needed and an order to them. The order has the time element as part of it, and that's easy to confuse with doing things in a hurry, which obviously is counter-productive. The 'just being' is an antidote to that and facilitates the jobs, in fact, because I have a relaxed attitude. When unexpected things crop up (the nature of jobs) I can make things happen/steer things the way I want them to go. It involves communicating with people on the way, often on the phone, and just being human really.

Rebalancing

I do need to flag up my own expertise, to be proud of things I can do. But now I feel I should modify that; acknowledge my weaknesses too – in relation to other people's strengths. It feels good to appreciate other people's strengths, to be reliant on others sometimes as well as self-reliant.

It seems counter-intuitive – the more confidence I get from the virtuous circle, the less I need to flag up my expertise and strengths, or my determination and will to succeed.

Over-confidence presupposes everything working according to plan, and it makes me say things like, 'It's got to work' or 'I'll make it work with my strength of will and purpose'. It would probably be more productive to say, 'It might not work', which, after all, is factually correct. Sometimes less is more. 'I'm going to try my hardest.'

It can be counter-productive to think in terms of success or failure. When I was an insomniac, being awake was failure to sleep – a bad night. When I slept, that was a good night – a success. Of course, to an ex-insomniac there's no such thing as a good or bad night's sleep.

I have found this extends to all areas of life. Success and failure are not absolutes. It's my attitude that counts. I choose my own wording. I have my own interpretation of what success is and how I use failure. It's a feel for balance that I've been using more and more, post insomnia.

Q. Looking for balance – doesn't that make you non-committal?

A. No, it's the opposite. Balance shows me the full spectrum, makes me more aware.

I think it's helpful to look at strengths and weaknesses in terms of a spectrum. Then I'm not limiting myself to being one thing or another. Is it really so hard and fast what we're like and how we are? Take being introvert or extrovert, sporty or academic – we're quick to label ourselves. But maybe we believe set things about ourselves which don't need to be set at all.

We label other people too and they do the same to us. But we don't like it when we're unjustly labelled. Labelling is bound to be unjust, though; it's always going to be inaccurate, unbalanced.

But it's possible to do some rebalancing. If I consider the whole spectrum, there may be more of a choice in it than I think. Looking back, as I found my way out of insomnia for good, I gained some valuable insights into this labelling thing.

As an ex-insomniac I gain confidence with my mind and also with my body. I feel like I have more choice about how I want to be. For me, it's like connecting up the introvert and extrovert sides of my persona.

I can approach life situations in the same way as I tackled insomnia, using the same tools and strategies. I know I have the ex-insomniac basics in place. I trust the confidence-and-control circle because it is based on evidence – feedback I give myself from my own experiences.

Yes it's nice to be busy, but somehow yesterday didn't work out as I thought it would – overshadowed by a couldn't-be-bothered mood. I want to use what I learnt yesterday – not sure how I can do that. It's all experimental – the Art course as well as myself! This is playing it by ear, trial and error, not being afraid to do it badly, to go along a false (unhelpful, unproductive) path. That can be just finding the day has been unproductive. You can't always be full of the joys of spring (and wouldn't want to be actually) and it's not always the highs that are productive. The lows tell you things too and bring about learning, maybe over a longer time frame, rather than instant and obvious.

In the virtuous circle I can be flexible. My mindset has space to grow. With insomnia I went round in circles. Stuck in a fixed mindset.

The confidence-and-control circle is both solid and flexible. An open-ended circle. That stable, balanced base gives me the confidence to trust my own judgment.

In my dream last night I wanted to give up the entire thing. I think it referred to my book. It was not as negative as it sounds though – more acceptance than frustration. I wanted to allow myself to fail but not see it as failure. And I still have that feeling now. I'm quite familiar with it – I had it with skiing at one point. It's up to me if I want to keep going, or not.

It seems paradoxical, but often you only know where you are with something when you've given it up. You see it from a different perspective then. Like me with skiing, you may end up carrying on with it anyway. But your take on it will have altered, moved on.

I learned from my insomnia turn-around that I can empower myself by switching positions. I can think something that may have been unthinkable previously. "I used to be an insomniac, but now I'm not."

From that self-reliant position – because it was up to me, my choice – I can more confidently tune in and feel my way to what I want to do next.

Everyone loves an encapsulation

I thought of another way of looking at being practical – making my life functional. We use 'dysfunctional', so why not 'keep my life functional'? It's a spectrum thing, a balance. The opposite would be imbalance, straying over towards dysfunction. My functional calm self has the feel of the virtuous circle about it.

I like the 'functional calm self' description of an ex-insomniac. It sums up all of the following:

> I'm learning and developing all the time. My post-insomnia progression empowers me. I make it my own. I find my own solution to my own problem. I cherry pick from my own mind as well as drawing upon what others think and say. I figure out what I want to ditch and what I want to switch to. I use my instincts. Tuning in with my ex-insomniac antennae, I favour refreshing thinking over tired thinking. I learn about myself, and that gives me a sense of progress, freedom and calm confidence.

I might throw in a 'creative' there: calm functional creative self. Yes, I like that.

And as an ex-insomniac I get a feel for connections and what is right for me. Things slot into place. I have found something sustainable; what I have been doing is working for me. So I want to do more of it. It's like practising a sport.

Q. Could you sum up what to do more of?

A. Here's a list of suggestions – things to do more of (because they work). First they worked in the sleep situation, and then they worked in my life generally. I'll group them into actions and activities of a similar nature:

> Turn emotional to practical/ say it doesn't matter/ leave it to my body/ keep nerves where I can see them/ tackle my own reactions

> Appreciate the present/ take the pressure off/ look for balance/ make things easier for myself/ challenge myself
>
> See the other side of the coin/ give myself feedback/ speak to myself with a mantra/ activate my spark of motivation

They are all ways of developing the ex-insomniac mindset.

Q. Can you put that mindset into a nutshell – one that applies to any situation, not just sleep?

A. Okay. Everybody loves an encapsulation (almost as much as an analogy).

Let me think. The nutshell will have to bring in the no-doubt mindset (I don't have insomnia anymore), sustainability (and it's permanent), delegating to my body (I let my body decide about sleep) and attitude to time (it doesn't matter if I'm awake).

Here we go. Some nutshell suggestions:

> I can be certain that, whenever I like, I can steady myself by being in the moment, focused on my mind and body as a whole.
>
> Practise allowing my body to take on feelings and emotions, so mind and body are working together.
>
> Everything's alright in each present moment – I can always tune into myself.

Slow down and tune in.

Remember to just be.

Be.

Reality is in the present

Slow down and tune in. Remember to just be.

I do that now, and it works well for me. I can be calm inside – I know what the extreme opposite of that is like. I know how horrible it feels inside when you lose the ability to be in the here and now. When I had post-natal anxiety, I was at the mercy of my nerves and could find no inner stillness. How ironic I was in a place called Peacehaven! I had no means then of reclaiming control, no steadying base to draw upon, as I have now.

I often take the beautiful coastal route from Brighton to Eastbourne and never think of stopping there, in Peacehaven, where we used to live. But one day for a change I decided I'd go for a walk there.

I parked up by Sainsbury's Local and bought sandwiches and a paper. I crossed to the cliff side of the South Coast Road and started walking towards the sea. First observations: windy, blustery, sun on the sea, white foam of the waves breaking onto the dark, wet shapes of the rocks and rock pools. Next the sounds: gusts in my ears and more distant crashing of the waves, walls of sound in layers, close by and background. Then the feel of the hot September sun on my head, my hands, through my jeans even. I'm walking along eating my sandwiches – pastrami on rye bread with emmental and salad – yes, I can taste the difference. I carry on along the cliff-top path to the Meridian memorial. A chap tells me that with GPS we know the nought-degree line isn't there, but a hundred yards away, just by his bungalow with the white picket fence.

What a difference it makes when you can appreciate the present – finding pleasure through the senses, seeking out interesting things, and enjoying chats with people!

This is where happiness lies, in the present. The reality – actually feeling happy – is in the moment. It has to be experienced for real, through the senses. You can't feel happiness theoretically, can you?

I came to realise that the past and future are composed of present moments. This was quite a breakthrough.

If I view my past in blocks of time, it turns into a dull, grey monolith, no detail to observe. Sand turns into crystals when you take a closer look; individual grains sparkle, don't they? Memorable, happy times I've had are the sparkling details, the moments I enjoyed.

Here's an example – a few lines from a poem about my dad:

Smartly dressed that day

My day. All caps and gowns outside, a lovely day

One day of many long ago

EQUILIBRIUM

That present day, mid conversation, chatting outside

I can recall feeling happy if I see it clearly in detail, how it felt – what my senses made of it at the time. Pleasure is in the detail, the moment – a recalled moment in the past or one I'm experiencing now.

And the ability to be in the moment sets me up for the same possibilities in the future, similar spontaneous feelings of happiness.

I know I will be in the moment when I'm walking home from the nursery later with H. I love tuning in to his world, sharing the excitement of pressing the button to light up the red man, then the bleeping green man, making sure we jump over the muddy bit.

When R asked me if I could pick H up (what a lovely question!) it wasn't a job to be done; I didn't race ahead in my thoughts. I could just be practical, knowing future times are composed of individual spontaneous moments. Confident in that knowledge.

How different that is from viewing my future as a planned and predictable block of time – projecting sameness, being set in my ways! I don't have to see it that way. It's up to me. Predictability is a mindset choice.

Q. But don't we need to see blocks of past or future time, in order to make sense of where we are in the present?

A. Yes, there's a balance point here. It's about combining detail with overview – having a functional, practical attitude to time. This, as we ex-insomniacs know, was key to ditching insomnia —

Time is a massive issue to insomniacs. To their minds, time awake in the night is endless and scary, an alien thing outside their control. But, as an ex-insomniac, I embrace time in the night. I am not afraid of it, because now I have made it my own. (Review of a sleepless night: 4)

It is all about getting a handle on what is real – in my own circumstances, using my own reference points; finding what will sustain me in living my life.

Q. But is it possible to know what is real? What can we base reality on?

It is one of the big questions about the human condition alongside why we are here.

All I can say is that my ex-insomniac mindset and practice has helped me to deal with struggles. When I might have been all at sea, at the mercy of my emotions, the tools and strategies have helped me to find a path that is right for me. I feel my way to the definite and practical, my own handle on what is real. I find doing these things helps with that:

> Tuning in to how things are, here and now
>
> Not trying to make them different to how they really are
>
> Taking on feelings, emotions, whatever reactions come my way

Proactively inviting them in; letting my body deal with them

I was just checking if the digitised version of the video worked and there before my eyes was my lovely family all those years ago and my mum with us then. I'm struggling with sadness – how do I process it? Let the past, the video, fade into the background (put it on the shelf and just know it's there, preserved). Come back to reality – the here and now – and move forward. Yes, use my ex-insomniac mindset. Be ready for this unexpected attack on my feelings. Invite the sadness in and explore it – bodily as well as thinking about it. The sadness is there – accept it, don't try to change it. Go with it – delegate it to my body – it's a way of living with it, not brushing it aside. Make it real and relevant to me now by bringing the feelings into the present moment.

Being in the here and now is my own individual experience of living. That's amazing, actually.

It was good advice in my diary yesterday – living with the sadness, not trying to make it go away. It really helped me. Plus, having my hair done and chatting to Gemma – about other things, e.g. she remembered I'd been on a writing course and it was therapeutic telling her about the experience and the difficulties. I walked in town too – before the hairdresser's (sat out in the sun with a sandwich) and after – shopped for food in M&S – just the right amount of bustle before coming home. I walked the long way round from the carpark via the woodland walk – beautiful view down the long tunnel of trees – and past the pond – a perfectly composed picture, quick treat for the eyes. And all just bringing the shopping home (the lime pickle leaked onto my trousers and I'm still trying to get the stains out).

Appreciating the present is a gift, it seems. How do I get it/ ensure it/ keep it?

I have to be able to switch my focus – sometimes to steady myself or remember to slow down inside – not only when there's a struggle of some kind, but in general living. Why? To stay a together person: mind and body functioning as one whole me. I find life's better that way.

Mind/body balance

As I see it now my accurate window on the world is not my conscious mind but my body as a whole. That is my window, my guide in the world.

I am my whole, together self. This knowledge and practice gives me confidence. A steadying inner confidence I can access, born of certainty of experiencing the here and now. This is where the spark of motivation is.

Best to get going and get out, even though the motivation for it isn't really there. I really do feel like wallowing – why not carry on allowing myself the sadness? Because it's melancholia now and you're slipping into a vicious circle. You can feel the difference, can't you? The way onto the virtuous circle of confidence and control – where you want to be – is to act. Do something.

I did. I still wasn't full of the joys of spring but during the day I went with the feelings and intrusive thoughts, using strategies and tools as and when. I wrote down these notes:

I have to acknowledge the feelings, allow them and deal with them.

Get my head into it. Recognise the vicious circle as it starts and steer myself away from it. Use my mind for problem solving.

Get my head out of it. Allow my body to take on the feelings. Then my head doesn't misread them and go racing off with them, making all sorts of unhelpful connections.

The key is sensing the vicious circle at work. Then the ex-insomniac basics come into play. That's reassuring because I know it works.

Q. What are the basics in general life?

A. Going from the vicious to the virtuous circle. The Insomnia Ditch-and-Switch

Q. How?

A. Head into it and head out of it. Mind and body working together.

Thank goodness I know a vicious circle when I see one. I know what a virtuous circle feels like.

I've been ill with a cold and haven't had my normal energy. It's made me appreciate how energetic I usually am. Now I feel I want to reclaim my body's energy, its rhythm and flow, this amazing (but underused and undervalued) resource. I haven't been swimming for ages. I think my body has missed that – letting go, allowing free movement. I've been neglecting it, ignoring it almost.

But I've been too busy, haven't had the time, getting on with important things.

What rubbish! It's laziness masquerading as efficiency.

I get taken up with things always having to have a purpose. That's how my mind slips into side-lining my body. The balance between body and mind weighted towards the mind, towards thinking and over-thinking. Mind/body balance skewed.

But I'm an ex-insomniac, I should know this.

I do – I just forget sometimes. It's easily done when I'm busy. I don't forget when it comes to sleep. That's second nature – my mind always allows my body the free flow of sleep.

When I'm lost in sleep or play, I'm lost in flow and rhythm. This is pleasure that has its own intrinsic purpose. No other purpose required. My body knows this, feels its way towards this, when my mind's reins are off.

I know I love to dance but when do I give myself the opportunity? Hardly ever. I could join something/do a class. Or sing – if there's a choir where you don't need to be able to sing. Or act. Or snorkel in the swimming pool. Okay, I'll do that to be going on with. The acting I already do when I join in with the children on some pretend adventure. I'm in my element then.

Stop press: I have joined a Zumba class. I dance every Monday evening now!

The feel of the virtuous circle

I'll remember to notice things – birdsong, smells, and to do ordinary things slowly with focused attention – stacking the dishwasher maybe. Give myself space from thinking. Space in that sense is time, freedom from the time element. The freedom of being in the moment.

Tuesday. I obviously didn't give myself space from thinking – I just got so sad. I had this ball of sadness inside. Different from a heavy heart – more intense. I nearly cancelled the day out when I got the feel of M's low mood. But he changed his tone just enough for me to recalibrate and focus on being out and about in Brighton on Bank Holiday Monday. Fish and chips walking along on the pier. It was a temporary feeling of a normal nice day. I couldn't shake off the sadness. (It may be to do with getting the overview – seeing all the sad things all at once.) Anyway, the ball of sadness has gone this morning. Maybe that's because I did see it as a ball – something I could visualise inside my body – not thoughts and emotions reeling around in my head. That must have happened spontaneously. If it comes again, the intense sadness, my body (teamed up with my mind) will deal with it again. I'd delegated it without realising. That's comforting, reassuring. Everything's alright actually.

I remember a similar thing with the mobile phone saga, how the frustrations turned to a ball of stress in my gut. The stress content surely wasn't real but the stress feeling definitely was. How unreliable my gut must be for telling me what's important!

But when my gut and my brain work together as a team, a two-way thing: gut helping brain, brain helping gut, shared ownership, this has good, positive direction, the feel of the virtuous circle.

Q. What's this shared ownership?

A. It's another way of saying delegate to my body. My mind works with my body to take on the sensations, to focus on what is real and now. They share ownership of anger, stress, fear, anxiety, sadness, frustration, and so on.

What was it like before, when my mind and my body were functioning separately? We were going nowhere, me, my body and my mind, everything getting worse. It felt horrible, bad, hopeless, no end to the stress – gut and brain working against one another in a vicious circle.

Yesterday I felt my body was pulling me down – the sensations of physical stress were really quite unnerving: palpitations, ear noise and this muffled echo. Plus, I couldn't shake being annoyed with the theatre: forced to sit right up close to the actors and their over-the-top shouting instead of acting, the decibel level inappropriate for the space. How stressed was I! And it's left me feeling nowhere near fit enough for having friends round to dinner.

I'd found it hard to rest inside, lying awake for much of the night. My body seemed to have been attacked by the physical stress. It was very similar to insomnia – the physical stress and the self-perpetuating vicious circle. I was back there again. All shaky inside, some horrible adrenalin taking over my mind and my body – a two-pronged attack.

But of course it's different now – I am thoroughly armed with my ex-insomniac practice. I used the Ditch-and-Switch to find my practical voice last night and didn't allow stresses of the mind to take over – though they did try. It goes without saying that I can rely on my body to see to my sleep – that's never an issue these days (and never will be).

It's a case of pacing myself, being slow and calm inside while I'm doing everything. Let's put this being-in-the-moment thing into operation. I'm not ill – these sensations just need managing. It's not easy to be in the moment when there's so much going on and there's a need to race ahead to make preparations and plans and fit everything in. But it's important to have the intention to be patient and calm.

This is where my mantras will come in handy. Patience and calmness. "Process of gradualness", my dad used to say. Not too much thinking ahead – forget my trip to Harpenden just for now.

Okay, I'm going to enjoy the baking. I'll enjoy getting the fresh ingredients for my dessert and I will have the satisfaction of finally conquering my baking phobia (only half joking).

A very successful evening – really enjoyable. I forgot about feeling unwell and didn't even notice my muffled ears. The dessert was a triumph.

15
The Possibility of Change

Different thinking

Yes, we want to be practical and motivate ourselves. Of course we don't want to get stuck; we want to be open to the possibility of effecting a change.

The trouble is we like to hold onto judgments and narratives we've always had. Familiar lines of thinking are there for us to fall back on. A nice simple narrative, lovely. A set of memories to fit in with it, good. And safe, easy judgments, aired and re-aired to stand the test of time. Perfect.

Q. What's wrong with that?

A. It stops you moving on.

You continue in the same groove, safe but stuck. It may not seem like a vicious circle but it does when you get bogged down in it. It was like that when I was bogged down in insomnia. But a new way of looking at it moved me forward. Different thinking. The Insomnia Ditch-and-Switch.

Do you ever do those magic-eye pictures? I think it's a really good analogy for seeing things a different way. At first there's nothing but a load of random coloured shapes on the page.

Then I switch my focus. Nothing happens but I persevere – that is if I've done it before or I trust someone who's done it before. I'm half-expecting the eureka moment when it all falls into place. And it does. The image jumps out at me. In complete 3D reality. Magic! And the object that's just popped up stays there, solid and firm, as I move my eyes around the scene. Amazing.

I just had a magic-eye moment on top of the hill. I shut my eyes and allowed all the sounds to come to my notice (not thinking-notice but hearing-notice). I was beautifully in the moment, just being. If thoughts intruded, I led them away, so I could re-focus on the sounds. It was a different way of being up there on the bench. A new focus. And it's sustainable. I can do that any time I want.

I'd just been looking at some magic-eye pictures, which I hadn't done for ages. It reminded me so much of the turn-around magic of seeing insomnia in a different way. I wrote this in my diary about dealing with stress in the night:

That new perspective took away all the negative emotion. It was like magic. (Get the overview: 3)

In the night the thoughts and fears about not sleeping mesh in with the issues and concerns accumulated during the day. And it needs something powerful to turn things around when I'm bogged down with it all. Where can I get this power? Not on the internet or instore. I get it from myself. The power is in my mind-switching. (What about stress? 3)

Not getting stuck means changing something, seeing things a different way. Life will always throw up situations where I feel stressed, trapped in a vicious circle, going nowhere – on any level, big or small. But having felt the power of ditching insomnia I know what is needed – a new way of looking at the situation, a change of viewpoint.

It can be gradual biding my time or quick-change switching. There's a place for both.

With insomnia it had to be drastic. Ditch everything associated with it. Make it happen – turn it around instantly.

And here's another example of an instant thing to ditch and switch: my own tone of voice. The one I use to myself or when I hear myself speaking to another person in a certain way, using a particular tone of voice that's unhelpful, maybe corrosive even. I can alter it. Regardless of what's actually being said – the tone will do it. The change of tone goes directly to my unconscious mind and starts a chain effect that alters the feel of the interaction.

My friend was telling me the other day how she switches voice when she hears herself speaking to her young daughter in a tone she's somehow got into but doesn't like. It gave me confidence to hear that, especially when she used wording like 'switch'. (Could go straight into my book, I thought)

Sometimes it's more to do with playing things by ear. I have a plan in mind and it takes patience, keeping my nerve. There's an order to things to make something happen. Tailoring the plan to the situation is creative. There's creativity in biding my time, having faith in where I'm heading. That's how the ex-insomniac mindset brought sustainable, permanent effects.

Reinterpret

I can think how I want to think. I can switch mindset, think differently, if I choose. It's up to me. As I move forward along the ex-insomniac path it seems to inform more and more about life, about relationships, about myself and others, and the possibility of change.

It's liberating – mind-switching as part of a virtuous circle of confidence and control. There's freedom in being responsible for myself, which contrasts with the sense of burden I felt when I was in the vicious circle of stress and insomnia.

I came to realise, too, I can alter my interpretation of past situations. It is very reassuring to know it's just that – my interpretation and I can change it. I'm stuck if I believe what's happened has happened, so my view of it must stay fixed. There's no going forward from that stance. Just as there's no going forward if I believe insomnia is there and can't be changed.

As an ex-insomniac I know it's all about mindset. It's my interpretation that counts. It's how I look at it, my viewpoint. And that can be changed, shifted, altered, if I choose and I allow it.

I've found it really useful to say to myself, 'It's not set in stone'. It reminds me – I can change my mind if I want. Using my ex-insomniac skills I can decide what I am able to change and what I want to change. I can look back and interpret things in a helpful way. This is giving myself balanced feedback.

I'm surprised I slept last night. Usually sleep is pretty unlikely after an evening out like last night at the RW Christmas meal – so many conversations to potentially go round in my head. I suppose I'm much more relaxed within myself about what I've said, how I came across, etc. Now I think much less about myself and more about other people – how nice someone was, how successful the evening was from everyone's point of view. Now I don't think in terms of possible mistakes or things I wish I'd said/not said. I can be satisfied with whatever I said or did, trust myself that it all will have been okay, because I know I try to go out to other people. I don't have to try actually, as it's become a natural thing to do and I like doing it.

Call upon the ex-insomniac mindset

You help yourself, but not in a self-centred vacuum. It brings with it the peacefulness I've experienced before that comes from accepting and allowing, when that feels right for me. You find it gets passed on to others too – without trying. When you're going through emotional turmoil, this really helps. I've been able to take so much from my overcoming of insomnia. That experience feels like a godsend.

Obviously post insomnia, just as at any time in my life, I can be hit by difficulties. Things happen, part of the ups and downs of life. It might be a sustained period of stress, a succession of stressful situations, or a sudden problem afflicting me. I might end up feeling quite oppressed and overwhelmed.

But the reassuring thing is I don't have to stay feeling that way. I have felt the positive benefits of being an ex-insomniac – I can keep on using what I have learnt and experienced.

THE POSSIBILITY OF CHANGE

I can ask myself the question:

Q. What should I do right now to take back control?

A. Recruit my ex-insomniac mindset. Do something.

First, recognise the counter spark that's blocking my energy and motivation. Perhaps it's a feeling of being stuck or trapped, or the sense of being swamped, oppressed. Identify it for its potential corrosiveness. Name it. Identify and locate it at the same time. Bring it out into the open, uncover it, un-mask it.

→ Identify it

> *Right now I have the stuck feeling, ruminating that won't budge, set-in low feeling; verging on despair? No, but on the spectrum towards despair (am I in a vicious circle here?)*

→ Locate it

> *My jaw – where it hinges by my ear – a set-in expression is there. Also it seems like there's a similar set-in expression within my chest (not stomach, where nerves usually are located). Yes, it's very much there now I've located it.*

This is low mood discovered and uncovered, brought out of its hiding place where it does the damage. Fears lurk in the background of the mind. I can't think my way out of these feelings of sadness or despair. That will turn into over-thinking and even more ruminating.

It's nice to have these low feelings where I can see them, like nerves. This is quite a breakthrough.

→ Stay with it

It felt like a breakthrough because I didn't have to do anything more than keep close contact with the bodily sensations. No result was required. That is a strategy in itself, not trying to alter anything. Every time the heavy feelings returned I could immediately locate the sensations in my body and stay with them. I was allowing my body to deal with them. As an ex-insomniac I'm familiar with that – letting my body decide about sleep. I'm also familiar with finding this interesting, doing research on myself.

The best part is – it works. Of course the difficult situation doesn't magically disappear but my feelings of depression or anxiety do. Not always instantly. Often it's a process of gradualness. (Thanks again for that one, Dad) But I know from past experience that the unconscious healing threads have already been set in motion.

Monday. It's so exhausting – just a weekend in H'den – and only half of Sunday. Each stage with the children has its own particular challenges, but always the rewards are there the same. Also I had a stressful dream to do with teaching and woke up a bit of a wreck this morning. Where did that come from after all this time? It must have been sorting out the children squabbling – of course, that's it. No need to think beyond that. I'm glad I don't mix in perceived stress with the tiredness – that really has to be taken on board as a separate item, and it can be delegated to my body. Identify it by locating the bodily sensations. It works a treat. I'll do it now: not in my jaw this time or head at all, more in my chest and shoulders; yes, all in that upper part. The tiredness is exactly there. Let's see how that bit of knowledge translates itself into how I go about my morning —

Sudden recognition of feeling awful – a generalised feeling, almost an attack. I was caught by surprise. But I immediately switched to the part of my body I'd identified previously as where the tiredness is located. I ditched the sudden stress in my head and switched to the specific location in my body. Awareness was enough, nothing more was needed. I didn't notice it after that.

I think this is the message: I need to be able to reinterpret my gut fears; tune into them; not be misled by them; not heed them as reliable signals to inform my course of action.

But they can be very persistent. Gut fears expect to be in charge and to stop me tuning in. I have to be ready to break the misleading links they have created in my thinking. Not easy when my brain has become programmed to expect a connection.

I certainly didn't take any notice of the stress from my dream. What a mistake that would be to heed some network in my brain that's been unnecessarily reactivated!

Mistake: "What is behind the dream? Why has teaching cropped up out of the blue – does it mean I'm still stressed about it? What's caused it? Maybe I'm more affected by it than I thought."

Ex-insomniac: "Old network no longer needed, thank you, brain. Let's ditch it, shall we? Don't let's have unhelpful associations. Okay, I know you work surprisingly slowly sometimes, so I'll be patient with you."

Tuning into my brain is way better than rushing into my gut's version of how to act. But not over-thinking. I can divert the potential havoc by focusing on my body's reactions and I won't bother asking why.

I've found it works better not to do causes or triggers. Instead, just deal with being awake on a practical level. It works for me – it's made me into an ex-insomniac, so I'm happy with that.

I won't ask why I've had a stressful dream about teaching, or why changing my phone got to my nerves. I don't do reasons and causes with things like that. I deal with my stress on a practical level.

Finding the path

We're all human beings in the same boat and not finding it easy. We can't avoid having to make assessments, adjustments, and changes in the course of living our lives. And we have conflicting elements in our psyches that make all these things frustratingly difficult.

We live with paradoxes – within ourselves and in relation to others – and we must deal with them. We like to be ourselves, to be unique and different, but at the same time we have the human urge to fit in. We have a need for adventure; we don't want to miss out on what others have or what others are doing. But at the same time we seek (our own version of) normality.

It helps if we tune into these kinds of duality, which we all have in one way or another. The inner conflict can lay dormant and then at some point in life manifest itself as stress or crisis. It's really important to have strategies, mechanisms at hand for dealing with stress as and when it arises in our lives in whatever form.

Bit by bit, as I get on with my life and use my ex-insomniac practice, I sense what makes it easier, more interesting, and less stressful for myself. I tune in to what to ditch and what to switch to. I get a sense of something to be changed or something to be left – often it's a case of doing nothing. Situations crop up in my life where I have to figure out what I can or can't control; what to accept or not accept; what to settle for, and adapt to, or not settle for.

Q. What is the place of accepting, of settling for something? Surely that can be a negative thing.

A. Yes, compromise goes both ways; it can be positive or negative, depending on the mindset that goes with it. There's a spectrum here.

I'll try and set out this positive-negative spectrum as a table. It might work:

Settled

Positive	Negative
Relaxed	Acceptance of boredom
Able to enjoy the moment	Settling for an unsatisfactory/unacceptable situation
Finding things interesting	Neutral feeling

Unsettled

Positive	Negative
Seeking interest	Bored
Wanting to problem solve	At the mercy of adrenalin
Recognising you're stuck	Nervy
Ready to change something (move into a virtuous circle)	Being stuck/trapped (vicious circle)

Boredom is potentially corrosive. We use the word 'boring' all the time, so its significance is lessened for when it's something quite deep. Real boredom is something that affects and attacks the soul. But I don't go around saying every time I find something boring that it's attacking my soul.

Boredom comes out of circumstances and from within myself, a mixture of the two. Balance and tuning in are needed. It's about getting an overview – an awareness of my outer circumstances and my inner reaction to them.

Ernest Hemingway coined the phrase 'crap detecting'; my ex-insomniac antennae are my crap detectors. They constantly need to be tuned up and reactivated. Why? To make life easier. With them I can detect the negative in my own thinking, then know what I want to ditch. There was massive negativity going on with insomnia and the thinking fuelling it. Crap detecting shows me the vicious circle so I can get out of it, not be stuck there.

Feel my way. Tuning in can be instinctive, conscious, both. Change something on purpose or leave alone. I seek to find the path that, for me, reduces stress. Tune in first. Then modify my thinking, use balance or spectrum to sort the positive from the negative and re-find equilibrium – with choices in life or on a day-to-day level.

Don't want to feel rushed and late. Want to look forward to getting the train and meeting R in London for lunch. I just need to relax, be in the moment, do everything slowly but getting on with it. It's a case of being calm inside while doing active things – washing hair etc. – and watching the clock in a non-panicky way. I have this groggy, unrelaxed feeling after being awake in the night and then sleeping on in fits and starts after the alarm this morning. I knew I had a bit of leeway with the time but I took too much. That is quite a stressful sort of sleep. Anyway it helps to observe it and I'll find my equilibrium as I get ready. I know how important that is.

Finding the path that reduces stress and fosters equilibrium means feeling my way with boredom and routine with work and in home life.

There are useful routines and unhelpful ones. Some routines entrench perfectionist patterns of thinking and behaviour. It happens a lot – at work and at home. It's a hiding to nowhere. I know this from my insomnia days. My sleep environment routines, though they promised security and control, were really a trap. Everything had to be just right. The routines seemed trivial at first. They crept into my life quite innocently, and then insidiously took over. I'm not exaggerating. They became the be-all and end-all. I strove to fulfil them and ended up mistaking my routines for my goals. Thank goodness I ditched all that. It was so tedious, way too much trouble for what it was worth.

Striving to reach our goals, accomplishing our tasks, can lead us into patterns which create a negative build-up, a vicious circle. Enjoying life becomes irrelevant. We must multitask; we must endure. The characters in the Necklace show us the big mistake of enduring. I endured insomnia; that was before I realised I could ditch it. Ditch enduring.

Routines are fine sometimes. And, more than that, we need them for the smooth running of our day-to-day lives. A routine frees me up because I don't have to think about it. It takes off the pressure of having to plan ahead, so I can relax in the present.

Tuning in is needed to identify the positive and negative in my own routines. Looking back, I was using my ex-insomniac antennae when I wrote those snorkelling notes on the beach.

I ditched the tyranny of routines. Small changes add up to a big difference, I noted. Once I'd identified the routines as fussing I could ditch them – and ditch fear of snorkelling into the bargain.

My antennae have detected negative routines in different guises. They have reported back with the following recommendations –

> Ditch fussing.
>
> Ditch being set in your ways.
>
> Otherwise you might not realise you're following your own time-worn patterns. You might entrench little fears which lead to bigger fears. Then you might get used to avoiding challenging situations rather than confronting them.

Okay, I think I'm doing quite well with that.

Now I find myself changing things just for the sake of it. Not big important things – just little things. Doing things a different way, changing my mind off the cuff, changing the order of how I usually do things, e.g. sitting in a different place in Pilates. Simply because it's refreshing – it has a different feel to it and I notice things when I'm in a different place or doing things a different way. Familiar things feel a bit odd, a bit new, a bit more unusual – special even. It gives my brain a little kick to sit up and notice this for a change. It's good for me. It means I'm flexible (Pilates is so good for that!), not set in my ways.

Sometimes I think I've learnt things, then find I haven't learnt them at all. There is no template. I have to keep reactivating my ex-insomniac antennae.

It's tempting but not helpful to think there's a ready-made template for putting right each situation, if just I could find it or consult the right person.

I think it's more a question of cherry picking, finding the path that's right for me, creating and re-creating my own way of looking at things. That's a balance of my instincts and my conscious figuring things out. I draw upon the wisdom of others and use my own savviness, playing things by ear. I sense what I can and can't control, dealing with stress in all its fascinating forms.

Tuning in. It's my individual creativity at work. Behind-the-scenes networks in my brain are making new connections, stimulating my creative thinking. It's a constant and interesting thing, figuring out what I want to ditch and what I want to switch to. It does feel good when something is right for me.

Get a sense of it

I expect you remember John saying on the beach, "I'm so cold I can't stop shaking". Then "No I'm not!"

I told you how in the middle of the night I did a similar thing: "No, I'm not. I'm not emotional". The Insomnia Ditch-and-Switch.

Did it sound impossible to you? If you get a sense of it, you're halfway there – to doing it yourself. Get a sense of what? In this case a sense of making a significant change. Turning from having insomnia to not having it.

Generally the phrase 'get a sense of it' is used for something you can't quite figure out now. But, instead of thinking I don't get it and that's that, I take in the idea of it, knowing I'll get it in due course. It's about allowing instead of dismissing an idea.

Perhaps you will come back to it later.

I write things in my diary and they turn out later to mean more than I thought they did at the time. But something made me write them – a sense of something. I was tuned in without realising or understanding at the time.

When I was in the throes of personal upheaval, I became highly conscious of strong conflicting forces within myself. But alongside the turmoil I got a sense of something else. I had the feeling that the difficult situation I found myself in was significant and I would learn important things from it about life and about myself.

Being an ex-insomniac and knowing that my emotions can be controlled has been invaluable to me. And this ex-insomniac knowledge led me to make another really helpful connection: feelings can't be forced, in the same way that sleep can't be forced. You just have feelings and need to tune into them.

I had a reasonably nice day yesterday, treating myself to a day out. I got the train to Eastbourne and milled around with the crowds, doing bank holiday things. I wasn't trying to make myself feel great – I was simply tuning in to how I was feeling. That does have a much better effect because you can't force your feelings. Sometimes it's not a question of doing a turn-around with your emotions. Recognising that seems really important and makes difficult times less stressful. I can give myself nice times without the expectation of feeling great or having improved mood. Not expecting a result really takes off the pressure.

I had wanted to make sense of the idea that I can turn myself from emotional to practical, but also that I can't force my feelings. No point in trying to have them or not have them; they are just there. I knew this was very much connected with what I'd figured out for myself about sleep. I can tune in to my feelings and, as with sleep, have a sense of how they are a natural occurrence.

Heeding my feelings but not being at the mercy of my emotions is another example of balance. I realised it was about getting a sense of what I can alter and what I just allow. Guess what – I feel another table coming on:

Alter	Allow
Insomnia	Sleep
Emotional	Feelings
Practical	Natural
Decide not to allow	Can only allow

Take control	Tune in
Try	Accept
Practise	Don't try
Problem solve	No solution needed

All this is about finding balance and learning for myself what I alter or allow. It's about tuning in to my own learning, getting a sense of what might be a learning experience. We often learn from difficult situations, it seems. Suffering from insomnia is a good example of that. I don't always know at the time when I'm learning something significant about life.

16
Sustainable Path

Spark activator

It's good now and again to experience an almost sleepless night for the sake of research! Calmness about it is key – and moving on as soon as I can to thinking of the day ahead. And knowing I'm not ill – I'll be fine. Accept the physical sensations that come with not feeling great and observe them. I will do it this morning because I know it works.

Knowing it works is another way of saying it's sustainable. I have my safety net of confidence. I can draw upon it.

I will need to draw upon it because difficulties crop up and my virtuous circle is not a permanent state. (I am a human being.)

I realised last night I could allow myself to feel flat, having some faith that it was just temporary. I did a trial spark activator: smiling to myself. It was more a fake smile actually – just to keep the balance, not to expect anything from it. I know the working of it has to wait a bit sometimes.

Q. What's this 'spark activator'?

A. When I lack motivation, I'm so flat I can't act – that requires motivation. This is a vicious circle at work. Somehow I need to reactivate my spark. Here's my diary with an illustration of it:

> *I'm suffering from low, flat mood. The smallest-possible action for me right now is to smile. Don't call it Step 1 (that means the first of many – too daunting). No, just a single step on its own – a very small one*

Q. How does it work?

A. I smile and I'm leaving it to my body. The rest will follow without me having to do anything at all. I have put optimistic brain activity in motion. The interweaving threads go to work behind the scenes beyond my conscious mind, sending positive messages to the unconscious part of my brain. This simple action – a smile – is activating the spark of optimism and motivation. It's small and simple. I am smiling. Everything's alright.

Spark activators have to be small and instant – the least possible effort for when I seriously can't be bothered.

Q. But if you're really that flat how do you even see the possibility of making a change in the first place?

A. I can think of two visualisations I have for that eventuality:

> 1. Magic-eye pictures (I mentioned them in the last chapter):

At first there's nothing but random coloured shapes. Then I switch my focus and the image jumps out at me. I can change the way I'm looking. I can do it in an instant.

2. I have this visual mantra from snorkelling:

When I'm snorkelling I can look either above or below the water's surface. By simply tipping my head I can see two different views through my mask. When I look down below I feel like I'm flying. When I look up above the surface I feel slow and heavy in comparison. I can change my view with a nod of my head – as I wrote in a poem while on holiday in Crete:

Two worlds with a tip of the head

Break the surface leave that world but oh! to be back

In a nod I'm flying again

Swimming like a bird at home with the fish

I can change the way I'm looking. I can do it in an instant.

This change of view/spark activator thing works for me. When the idea of doing a Ditch-and-Switch is like climbing Mount Everest, a small smile is all I can manage. But it's something. And it's enough. It doesn't take much – just enough to start the ball rolling in a positive direction. It might be obvious or scarcely perceptible but it's there and it's working. My faith in it only needs to be vague and in the background. No more than that.

A bit savvy

Author's note: Sorry about this sudden burst of poetry, but I was looking back over the poems I've written and this line jumped out at me: *the brain can wait; it has been boss for far too long.* It said exactly what I want to say next – about giving my brain a rest.

I wrote the poem after a holiday on a canal boat. Over the course of the week I had gradually relaxed into the slower pace. I was relaxed enough to allow my eyes, my ears, my nose – my senses – to take over.

As the boat chugged closer to the end of a long tunnel I watched the picture created by the light and the shape. I wasn't looking in a literal way. I didn't ask myself, 'What exactly is that?' In this quite special atmosphere of relaxation I didn't need to know. I could enjoy it visually.

> *Chugging in a dark kaleidoscope tube*
> *towards the end light, what is depicted there?*
> *indiscernible, intriguing; relaxed enough*
> *to read it visually, the brain can wait;*
> *it has been boss for far too long.*

My conscious mind was badly in need of a rest. I gradually realised this as I felt more and more relaxed. It was a transformation. I was a different person:

I'm different here
my eyes, my body, my mind
shifted, adjusted, reinterpreted

What a relief for my brain! Without tiresome interference and explanations from my conscious mind, my unconscious mind could relax into these pleasurable experiences.

Q. So how do you give your brain a rest in life generally (when you're not on a canal boat)?

A. I create opportunities for myself where I may have an interesting, enjoyable experience; where I may be lost in play, lost in music, lost in sport; where I may be absorbed, fascinated, rapt; where I can relax, slow down, switch off.

Make it my own. Create opportunities for myself, ones I know I'll enjoy. Or I may not know beforehand. It may be a spontaneous thing that grips my attention. I might not have realised I'd enjoy it. Opportunity relies on spontaneity. Spontaneity relies on opportunity.

Q. So does this mean we can positively affect our unconscious mind?

A. Yes

I know this from dealing with insomnia –

I can't directly control my unconscious mind (by definition) – only indirectly. My instincts about insomnia tell me not to do causes, triggers. Instead of trying to work it all out, I let my body be in charge. I consciously have my ex-insomniac mindset and allow my unconscious mind to look after sleep.

I relax by turning emotional to practical, by making insomnia interesting (seeing myself as a fascinating case study), by establishing my no-doubt mindset and using my own mantras. I rest and let my body be in charge of sleeping, leaving underlying reasons for previous insomnia to evaporate.

I am setting in motion the interweaving threads behind the scenes, the ones that go towards creating optimism, peacefulness, motivation. These benefits are not fleeting, but sustainable. Compare this:

… you are left with something much more tangible, not fleeting like sleep; you are left with insomnia. It seems to have a will of its own, nothing to do with you. And it's frightening. You are at its mercy, no matter how rational a person you might be. (Insomnia does not exist 1)

How the tables have turned on insomnia!

I've got to be a bit savvy when it comes to my unconscious mind. Savviness is being practical, functional, and creative – giving myself pleasurable experiences on purpose which will do their work inside my brain.

It's therapeutic – setting optimism in motion to go on working behind the scenes, in passing, without me thinking about it. It's nourishment for my psyche. How different that is from being scared of my psyche, feeling it's something independent of me, beyond my control. That's horrible. What a different attitude to my psyche I have now!

Being a human being

Q. Sorry to burst the bubble, but sometimes my psyche goes out of my control. What attitude can I have then?

A. Yes, being a human being, that happens. It won't be any surprise to hear that I have the ex-insomniac take on that.

I'll tell you about an emotional outburst I had recently. It was during a skiing holiday with the family.

"I can't believe nobody came out to find me. I've been waiting ages out there and you're all in here eating. Didn't you wonder what I was doing? I'd have thought one of you could have come out to see where I was. What's the use of making arrangements?" R tried to defend himself and made me more annoyed with them all. Their behaviour towards me was indefensible. Treating me so badly. It was what it was – how dare they try to make it otherwise. I wouldn't be feeling this bad if I hadn't been so blatantly mistreated and ignored. Then J sussed out it was best not to argue with me, but to give me a seat at the table with something to eat and drink and a small hug.

I hadn't realised stress had been building up inside me, I thought I was fine up to that point. I'd been under some stress but I was using my ex-insomniac strategies, as I do, taking the pressure off myself as I went along.

But I was suddenly overcome, like being hijacked. I couldn't help it. Even though the crowded restaurant would witness my outburst, the stress inside me had to come out. My anger and frustration burst out of me like an explosion. Okay, I just lost my temper. But it was the way I was temporarily out of control, not my manageable self at all. I'm going to be honest here – it was consuming, overpowering, an unforeseen and unstoppable loss of maturity and rationality. Like a teenager, or a toddler having a tantrum. I didn't intend to be like that. No, I hadn't chosen it. I didn't want to be saying those words or using that tone of voice. But I couldn't help it.

So, what can I learn from this? What will my attitude be?

I remember how this anguished outburst felt at the time. Anguished? Surely that's going over the top. No, I've been here before. My brain-gut nervous system does this to me from time to time. It doesn't recognise any difference between serious and trivial things. Real anguish or false pseudo anguish – I'm attacked just the same.

I couldn't avoid the outburst. I was taken unawares. My emotions took over and no control was possible for a while. It happens.

It reminded me of when I was at the end of my tether with insomnia and I couldn't contain my emotions any longer. I remember the eruption. I understand it. I understand myself in that situation.

The thing is to make it useful to me. How? It's afterwards that I can make rational choices. I choose, for a start, not to heed the content. I didn't really have any grievances against my family. What I could do afterwards was to let everyone off the hook, including myself. It wasn't good or bad; I didn't need to make any judgment on myself, or on anyone else. Ditch blame. That's no use to anyone.

I choose how to view this sort of occurrence, so I can be better informed next time. The experience, along with the tools or strategies, will be in my locker.

I'm in charge, reviewing what happened, using it for feedback and learning. I will gain strength from it, not see it as weakness or failure. I'm taking on the stress as I took on the insomnia.

Plus, it's all very interesting.

Alright whatever

I thought of another way of looking at this virtuous circle I've been talking about: a support framework. As I gathered my strategies and found I could keep using them in day-to-day living, I realised I was building a framework. I had a pathway to confidence and control: the Ditch-and-Switch mechanism with the Ex-insomniac Mindset behind it. I could rely on it. It was sustainable.

It's up to you what you call it: a support framework, a safety net, a life jacket maybe. It's about using over and over again the learning experience of ditching insomnia and becoming an ex-insomniac. Altering your angle becomes a transferable skill and it comes in very handy.

Tuning into my body has sustainability. I can be in every present moment – at will. I can delegate nervousness, sadness, any emotion I like (or don't like!) from my mind to my body

I can get my head out of it by switching location; switching from my head to my body.

I did this switching from head to body previously with breathing:

The other day someone told me how he relaxes when he's not sleeping. He said he concentrates on his breathing and doesn't let any other thoughts take away that focus. Relaxation techniques didn't work for me when I had insomnia. They just made me more aware of not being asleep and more frustrated – so I ditched them along with insomnia. But now I could use that breathing focus idea in my own way, while I rested, alongside not minding being awake and leaving sleep to my body.

I've used this focus on breathing quite a lot since then – at any time. My breathing seems like the first port of call for tuning into my body. It's the easiest, most instant and direct channel.

I can channel all that horrible ruminating stuff into my body. How great is that! I can let my body take things on that my mind has been finding so difficult to bear: stress, fear, sadness, frustration, anger, worry.

My body and my mind are much more inter-connected than I ever realised. Ditching insomnia showed me this – letting my body decide about sleep. I found I could use this idea more and more. It may not be obvious – this ruminating stuff in my mind being connected to sensations in my body. I have to practise tuning in.

It pays off. And, into the bargain, I'm switching to the present moment. My thoughts will have been racing ahead to the future, all mixed in with ruminating on the past. When I leave it to my body, I settle myself in the present. How obvious – that's where my body is, the present!

I will always be able to do that, delegate to my body. So I'll be alright whatever. It's empowering to know that.

Looking back – questions

Okay – looking back to the beginning and coming round full circle:

> Everyone has sleeplessness, so how did I become a chronic insomniac?
>
> How does equilibrium return over time?

And answers (in a nutshell: promise – I have just written a whole book on it!)

> I fell into the pattern of the vicious circle. Sleeplessness – stress – sleeplessness – stress (I could go on but it's rather boring.) I had no strategies (none that worked) to deal with it, so insomnia was left free and wild to perpetuate itself.
>
> You break the circle once (aha!) – the Insomnia Ditch-and-Switch – then use mantras to keep the Ex-insomniac Mindset going. Equilibrium returns over time without you planning it or even noticing.

I enjoyed the meal out at The Plough with M, just pleasant and easy. I feel the stress sensations are gradually abating, a return of my equilibrium. Normality really – bodily normality. It's a fine thing. It happens over time – just like insomnia.

Finally

Well, there it is. My book is finished. I had been wondering if I could ever end it, as it's all so ongoing. But I have and I'll say goodbye to it now, leaving it on the theme of a sustainable path.

I'll just allow myself a final couple of Q & As:

Q. What was the book for?

A. Basically, it's been me figuring things out and passing things on – things about being human and being with others in the world. The book is my communication with a reader who may, or may not, be imaginary.

Q. Where does it go from here, I wonder?

A. The answer depends on you, dear reader, and whether you are real. How crazily existential is that!

Anyway, it's been interesting for me writing it and I guess it's been interesting for you reading it. You seem to have read right to the end. Good, I'm glad about that.

If you are a real person I wish you farewell, good journey. Truly, have a nice day.

End note 1

In the book I have quoted from poems I wrote about some nice times I've had. Here are the complete poems if you'd like to read them:

The Photograph (Reality is in the present: 14)

So sad
He's there. Living, breathing, smiling
Smartly dressed that day
My day. All caps and gowns outside, a lovely day

So proud
He's there. His face, his look, his stance
One day of many long ago
That present day, mid conversation, chatting outside

So happy
He's here. Familiar, loving, warm
That day is now, here, with me
Every day the continuity, my dad

* * *

Snorkel Expedition (Spark activator: 16)

Two worlds with a tip of the head
Break the surface leave that world but oh! to be back
In a nod I'm flying again
Swimming like a bird at home with the fish
Breathing in rhythmic flow surveying the scenes
Layers of rock like tiers on a cake-stand yes! its handle on top
Now strata tipped up standing in stage-set layers
And random sculptures jagged craggy shapes
Waves lap against my snorkel in the other world
More alien than this the sunlight shapes and moves the water
Against stillness of the rocks and shoals of flitting fish
Black like the urchins clustered in crevices
A blue-striped ochre-yellow one swims through a channel
Sides of grassy seaweed salt-tinged white
I follow along high above the seabed sand
Gliding with giant's ease small between the landscaped rocks
Ahead huge tessellating slabs smoothed boulders and
Man-made, look! Hand-crafted stone of ancient Olous
Lying earthquake strewn millennia long in light-bathed shallows . . .
Arrival by snorkel: we're fish out of water
[Human holiday activity: taverna, retsina, sardines]
Departure by snorkel: oh to get back in! Fluid again

* * *

END NOTE 1

Breathing Space (A bit savvy: 16)

High-speed Virgin bullets past. Unmoved
we sail, the M1's concrete underbelly
ceilings our space. Elatedly calm
we glide our *American Thrush*
proud in canal painted livery

Lynda greets a passing fellow knitter
on matching barges' patios;
in harmony the narrowboat and I
controlled that passing; I lean on the tiller
her sixty-foot length bends in response

It's addictive this power; as confident and
serene as mallards and their brood
we tootle along and magic ourselves
into paintings' infinite greens
pointilliste bridge circles

Chugging in a dark kaleidoscope tube
towards the end light, what is depicted there?
indiscernible, intriguing; relaxed enough
to read it visually, the brain can wait;
it has been boss for far too long

I'm part of the rhythm of Foxton Staircase;

finding my body's fulcrum I push or
pull, the will to move a mountain
or sit on the gate-arm to wait, my bottom
in communion with the levelling water

O, sweet irony, the locks have unlocked
this person: acquirer of waterway skills
lock mechanics appreciator
sluice-gate enthusiast
carrier of windlass

I'm different here
my eyes, my body; my mind
shifted, adjusted, reinterpreted;
to this my transportation transmutation
bear witness if you will

* * *

And I thought you might like to see the story I read out at the writing course —

The Passenger

Ole Bill had changed. The fondly-named London omnibus looked completely different. The distinctive bright-red livery had been painted over in khaki, the windows boarded up, and the shiny Fuller's Earth advertiser's hoarding removed. All these changes, however, could not conceal Ole Bill's unmistakeable appearance: the open-topped double-decker with curved staircase at the rear; driver's cabin and conductor's platform, front and rear, open to the elements, reminiscent of the horse-drawn vehicles Fred Crumsall had driven as a young man.

Fred remembered when Dottie would wait at the Seven Kings terminus with some piping-hot tea. He was that cold his hands could not grip the mug and his lips were too numb to take a drink. Thinking back now, that was nothing compared to this. He had Dottie's blessing, though; that was the main thing. She was proud of him for volunteering to do his bit for the war effort; he would not let her down.

'All aboard. One at a time.' Fred heard Alf's familiar voice. 'Move along the deck. That's it, boys.' They had always run their route like clockwork, Fred and Alf, the two Alfreds, driver and conductor. They had the same dedication to duty, wearing their LGOC regulation uniform with pride. The white greatcoat had been replaced by the khaki military issue, as was to be expected, but the all-important insignia of the Omnibus Service remained unchanged.

'Always the same, ain't it, Tommy? You waits hours for a number 47, then three turns up at once,' complained one of Fred's new passengers. Fred felt like giving them a piece of his mind, but held his counsel. He was not a dour man; he could take a joke. And, by Jove, these lads could do with having their joke. Ole Bill, now in service with the Auxiliary Omnibus Companies Association, was about to ferry these men to the front line on the Ypres Salient.

Alf shouted his report to Fred: 'Full complement of passengers, Driver.' It had always been 18 on top, 16 inside. Now with fully-equipped soldiers, it was 25 passengers all told.

'Yeah, no overloading – mustn't put us self in danger, eh, lads!' chimed up the joker in the pack. 'Hold on tight, boys, don't want any knocks and grazes before we even get there, do we now?' Unheeding, Fred called back to his conductor as per regulation, 'Prepare to move off.'

They had been through the routine countless times. But this was not route 47. You didn't take your vehicle to the depot at the end of your shift and pick it up in the morning, cleaned and overhauled. Nothing like that here in Flanders. You didn't turn up for work after a good night's kip. You bedded down at the roadside beside your vehicle. Every hour through the night you'd be cranking the old boy, so as he wouldn't seize up. No use to man nor beast if he wouldn't start. You even put hot embers under the sump if it was that cold.

Up till now their job had been to bring reserves up to the Front. Fred and Alf had become familiar over the months with the route from embarkation port to front-line positions. And familiar too with the job of ferrying the walking-wounded back to the hospital. Their job sometimes meant bringing one or two stretcher cases from the dressing station, if no ambulance was available.

'Come on, Ole Bill. You can do it.' A roar went up when the engine fired into motion and Fred said his usual silent prayer.

'Another stretcher job, Alf, this way. Let's get this one on, quick as you like, but for Gawd's sake be careful.'

END NOTE 1

'They should've got 'im to the aid post, not left 'im 'ere for the likes of us.'

'There's plenty worse than this one, Alf. Just your common-or-garden omnibus passenger, ain't ya, matey? We'll 'ave ya to 'ospital in no time.'

Fred scarcely seemed aware of the cloying mud and moved on to 'pick up his next passenger', as he'd say. He was surprised the ambulance team had not taken this one; he was obviously dressing-station priority. Then Fred saw the coarse grey cloth, the silver engraved buckle, and the muddied lettering: *Gott mit uns*. 'We've got another one over 'ere, Alf.'

Alf strained to drag the stretcher, heavy with mud, over mounds to the clayed-up hollow where the injured man lay. 'My Gawd, we don't take Germans, do we, Fred?'

'We're picking up passengers, ain't we, Alf. That's what we does, we treats all passengers with fairness and courtesy. LGOC employee code, Alf. Let's get 'im on the 'bus. We ain't got all day.'

'Full complement of pass....' Alf was not able to complete his conductor's report, due to a commotion on board.

'Get 'im off the 'bus, the lousy Kraut.'

'We're not savin' 'is life, when our boys are dyin' out there.'

'What the bloody hell are you thinking of? You've got no right...'

An omnibus driver must never leave his post at the wheel, save in defence of life and limb. Fred's authoritative frame rose out of its seat. The belligerent crowd parted, as his stubby hands sliced a furrow towards the dove-grey eyes pleading from the stretcher.

'Now look 'ere, you lot...pipe down and pay attention. By the power invested in me, Alfred Crumsall, by the Auxiliary Omnibus Companies Authority and under the jurisdiction of Army Command, I hereby order you to stand back.'

'Alfred Bickersthwaite, being my Second-in-Command, is hereby deputised to carry out guard duty on this 'ere passenger, and to report any contrary action to myself in person. Now every man back to his seat forthwith.'

Many people came up to shake Fred's hand and to admire his medal for Distinguished Service. He had received the highest commendation given to members of the Motor Transport Corps.

Furthermore, the King himself had for the first time boarded an omnibus, in order to carry out an inspection of Fred Crumsall's motor vehicle.

One figure in particular drew Fred's attention as he approached to join in the congratulations. It could have been because of the young man's uncommonly tall stature or his striking features, or perhaps it was a certain sense of recognition Fred felt. It was only when he saw the intensity in the young man's eyes that Fred recognised him as the German passenger on his

END NOTE 1

'bus in Flanders. 'Do you remember me, Mr Crumsall? The young man spoke softly but firmly, precisely.

'I did not at first, but I do now. My dear boy, to think what you looked like when we picked you up that day. But I can see that you is fit and healthy now. Look at you – fine figure of a man indeed. How did you get here?'

'I am here primarily because you gave me the gift of life. Because you looked beyond the enemy uniform and saw a man. That is what brings me here. And also the number 47 omnibus. I have business here in London, and was lucky enough to see the picture of you receiving your medal. I read about the King inspecting your omnibus, and so, here I am to thank you in person.'

Fred was overwhelmed. He had been presented with a medal by King George himself, and now this fine young man was honouring him with his words of gratitude. It was most humbling. 'I am glad I was able to help. Now, tell me, what do you intend to do in your life, my boy? Drive an omnibus like me?'

'No, Fred, I could never aspire to be like you. First of all I intend to marry my sweetheart, Emilie. I am a commercial salesman at present, but I want to try my hand at managing a business of my own, as soon as an opportunity arises.'

'Well, I wish you all the luck in the world, dear boy.'

'I will always remember what you did for me, Fred. Whatever happens in my life, I will never forget you.'

'Tell me your name before you go – Dorothy is bound to ask me.'

'It's Schindler, Oskar Schindler.'

* * *

And I couldn't resist the temptation to slip in a couple more of my poems. I've chosen ones that relate in some way to the ex-insomniac approach to life:

Flight over the Grand Canyon

parched-green Arizona scrubland
falls away
over the edge of the Rim
a breath-taking drop
down a mile-deep gorge
and sense-defying sight beyond
its vastness over-works the eyes
colours and forms attack the mind
my soul by an unfamiliar world
is transported

red terraces of ancient rocks
uplifted layers show off their
billion-year formation

END NOTE 1

the Colorado curves a cold-blue ribbon
carves into strata; imagine
before the massive rift
a huge plateau below the sea

flying is like snorkelling
from the surface I look down into deep water
survey the landscape beneath me
alone with the vastness
I witness its beauty

* * *

As I start my walk

As I start my walk birdsong appears
As if not there before I listened
A squawk-squawking slices through the other tones
Across and up and gone beyond the Downs
Leaving behind a different song, multiphonic
A canon of layers and levels far beyond my listening ear
In and out of focus, birds heard unseen. There
There is one I see and hear sharp in earshot

Down past the field, damp with rain and freshly cut, smell
                                                   overrides
'Til senses adjust and recombine; hearing renewed picks out
A rattling, chirping, almost squeaking, birds in flight

Passing, and some still, altering the timbre and the tone
Close-sounding voices shock my hearing
As riders in the distance semi-hidden
Show up the mismatch of my eye and ear
I laugh at my amazement

I focus on my breathing and my strides
Knowing at the top my view awaits
A bench looks out with joy, as Muriel would each day
Over the Downs to the sea, grey today but brightish
Gun-metal colour, satin finish, and the constant windmill's
                                              silhouette
A plane's low hum above the clouds shows me the panorama
                                              of the sky
Its variations, colour, cloud; I marvel at the textbook range
And sigh at my being here and now

* * *

Hi, Mum

Her spirit is with me
My mum, an ordinary woman
"Let's make it cosy. When we get in
We'll draw the curtains."

Baby's awake in the middle of the night
"You feed him, love. I'll make the Horlicks."
Just an ordinary woman, my mum

END NOTE 1

Our boy's got a lump on his back
Tests show its cancer but don't know what level
"I've prayed," she said
"That I'll have the cancer instead."
A miracle – first tests were false
Pseudo-carcinoma – benign. Benign!

Mum was happy in the hospice
"I don't mind being here," she said
"It's what I prayed for."
Just an ordinary woman, my mum

She made all the doctors laugh
"What a good invention, this catheter
Even better than the dishwasher!"

An ordinary woman, my mum
And her spirit is here. Hi, Mum

(Post Scriptum)
What do you think? Great granddaughters, twin girls
Born the same day five years later
The day you died. What joy you gave!
Thanks, Mum

* * *

You're there

I'm in your shoes, Dad
A generation later and I'm there

You idolised your little shiner
Following him around
Playing cymbals in his band

He made your day, Dad
Your little grandson made your life

Three years with him too little time?
That is not the way it was
Your glowing heart leaves time behind

I'm in your shoes, Dad
As I adore our baby girls

Patience flows freely unhampered by time
Each moment as precious as they
I know your heart soared and you're there

*　*　*

For Richard

When you were born
I kept the feelings in my heart
The quiet joy still here the same
Surges at the sight of these
Two tiny babies, each her own persona
As one, together in the basket
Sisters familiar from the womb
Snug asleep, an arm against a cheek

Daughters and granddaughters, children of my child
My own baby grown a man
These his girls, precious beyond the word
Beautiful, as beauty cannot comprehend
As my own son knew, so you will know
How you are welcome in this world
And you will grow and learn and love
As you are loved

End note 2

You may be interested in some of the books I was reading as I wrote Diary of an Ex-Insomniac. I like other writers to communicate with me. I see it as giving and receiving help, one person to another. In my book I call it cherry picking; this is what I like to do – taking from each book whatever connects with me. Sometimes I come back to a book and it relates to me more later on. It makes sense to me then and I can learn from it. It's important, this communication thing – we all depend on interaction. I have benefited from the scientific research of authors who are experts in their particular field. They led me to confirm or adjust my thinking and gave me the confidence to trust my ideas and experiences.

Black Box Thinking: Marginal gains and the secrets of high performance by Matthew Syed

The Blank Slate: The modern denial of human nature by Steven Pinker

Bounce: The myth of talent and the power of practice by Matthew Syed

The Brain that Changes Itself: Stories of personal triumph from the frontiers of brain science by Norman Doidge

Breakdown: A personal crisis and a medical dilemma by Stuart Sutherland

The Chimp Paradox by Prof Steve Peters

Depression: The way out of your prison by Dorothy Rowe

Happiness by Design: Finding pleasure and purpose in everyday life by Paul Dolan

The Inner Game of Skiing: Revised edition by W. Timothy Gallwey

Irrationality: The enemy within by Stuart Sutherland

Mindfulness: A practical guide to peace in a frantic world by Prof Mark Williams and Dr Danny Penman

Mindset: How you can fulfil your potential by Carol Dweck

The Philosophical Baby by Alison Gopnik

Reasons to Stay Alive by Matt Haig

Sane New World: Taming the mind by Ruby Wax

The Seven Basic Plots: Why we tell stories by Christopher Booker

Subliminal: The revolution of the new unconscious and what it teaches us about ourselves by Leonard Mlodinow

The Tipping Point: How little things can make a big difference by Malcolm Gladwell

The Upside of Irrationality: The unexpected benefits of defying logic at work and at home by Dan Ariely

Zen in the Art of Archery: Training the mind and body to become one by Eugen Herrigel

End note 3

The artwork on the cover came from a family activity inspired by Henri Matisse's cut-outs. Contributions are from: the adults, Richard and Julia, John and Sophia, Nicki and Martin; the children, Zara and Margot, and Henry, a toddler at the time, who painted the yellow background.

Made in the USA
Columbia, SC
14 November 2017